Transformative
Assessment

transFORMATIVE ASSESSMENT

w. james POPHam

Association for Supervision and Curriculum Development
Alexandria, Virginia USA

Association for Supervision and Curriculum Development
1703 N. Beauregard St. • Alexandria, VA 22311-1714 USA
Phone: 800-933-2723 or 703-578-9600 • Fax: 703-575-5400
Web site: www.ascd.org • E-mail: member@ascd.org
Author guidelines: www.ascd.org/write

Gene R. Carter, *Executive Director;* Nancy Modrak, *Director of Publishing;* Julie Houtz, *Director of Book Editing & Production;* Katie Martin, *Project Manager;* Reece Quiñones, *Senior Graphic Designer;* Marlene Hochberg, *Typesetter;* Sarah Plumb, *Production Specialist*

All Web links in this book are correct as of the publication date below but may have become inactive or otherwise modified since that time. If you notice a deactivated or changed link, please e-mail books@ascd.org with the words "Link Update" in the subject line. In your message, please specify the Web link, the book title, and the page number on which the link appears.

ASCD Member Book, No. FY08-6 (April 2008, PC). ASCD Member Books mail to Premium (P) and Comprehensive (C) members on this schedule: Jan., PC; Feb., P; Apr., PC; May, P; July, PC; Aug., P; Sept., PC; Nov., PC; Dec., P.

PAPERBACK ISBN: 978-1-4166-0667-3   ASCD product #108018
Also available as an e-book through ebrary, netLibrary, and many online booksellers (see Books in Print for the ISBNs).

Quantity discounts for the paperback edition only: 10–49 copies, 10%; 50+ copies, 15%; for 1,000 or more copies, call 800-933-2723, ext. 5634, or 703-575-5634. For desk copies: member@ascd.org.

Library of Congress Cataloging-in-Publication Data

Popham, W. James.
  Transformative assessment / W. James Popham.
     p. cm.
  Includes bibliographical references and index.
  ISBN 978-1-4166-0667-3 (pbk. : alk. paper) 1. Educational tests and measurements. 2. School improvement programs. I. Title.

  LB3051.P61447 2008
  371.27'1–dc22
                         2007049281

_____

19 18 17 16 15 14 13 12 11 10 09 08   1 2 3 4 5 6 7 8 9 10 11 12

Transformative Assessment

Preface

This is a book about classroom assessment, but it's not about giving tests. Really, it's a book about instruction, because classroom assessment can fundamentally transform the way a teacher teaches.

The foregoing paragraph, though modest in length, sets forth what some might regard as a meaningfully immodest aspiration. Any time an author predicts that a book can help bring about a *fundamental transformation* in anything, you're usually dealing with an author in need of reality therapy. Why do I claim this book about classroom assessment can trigger a fundamental transformation in someone's teaching? I do it because I believe that claim to be stone-cold true.

This book about the transformative power of formative assessment is written not for scholars but for educational practitioners, the teachers and administrators who staff our schools. If you are a teacher, here are the sorts of questions I hope you will be able to answer after reading this book:

- "What is formative assessment?"
- "Should I try to use formative assessment with my own students?"
- "If I decide to use formative assessment, how can I do so in a way that is *most likely* to benefit my students?"
- "Are there different variations of formative assessment I should implement in certain situations?"
- "If I use formative assessment appropriately, will my students' scores on external accountability tests improve enough so that I can stop taking tranquilizers?"

These questions are important ones. But the most important question waiting for you to answer is this: "*Should I set out to fundamentally transform my instructional approach with a significant infusion of formative assessment?*"

Just so you won't be blindsided later on, I'll make my bias known now. Yes, I think you most definitely *should* try to transform your instructional approach by incorporating formative assessment. I think you should do this because your students will almost certainly benefit as a result. And benefiting students is why most of us went into the education game in the first place.

Before you start digging into the book's seven chapters, I want to give you a brief overview of what's coming. In Chapter 1, we'll cover not only what formative assessment actually is but also why it is receiving so much attention these days from educators throughout the world. In Chapter 2, we'll look at the key to well-conceived formative assessment: *learning progressions,* the carefully sequenced sets of subskills and enabling knowledge that students need to master on their way to mastering a more distant curricular aim.

With this foundation information established, it's on to Chapters 3 through 6, each of which focuses on a different application—or "level"—of formative assessment available for educators' use. Why subdivide formative assessment into different levels? That's a reasonable question. Put simply, there is considerable confusion among educators regarding the nature of formative assessment. Many are still confused by how formative assessment bears on the day-to-day activities of teachers, students, and school administrators. So, for clarity's sake, it seems prudent to break out formative assessment into functions that are fundamentally distinguishable from one another:

- Level 1 calls for teachers to use formative assessment to collect evidence by which they can adjust their current and future instructional activities.
- Level 2 deals with students' use of formative assessment evidence to adjust their own learning tactics.
- Level 3 represents a complete change in the culture of a classroom, shifting the overriding role of classroom assessment from the means to compare students with one another for grade assignments to the means to generate evidence from which teachers and students can, if warranted, adjust what they're doing.
- Level 4 consists of schoolwide adoption of one or more levels of formative assessment, chiefly through the use of professional development and teacher learning communities.

After you've become familiar with this four-level split, you can decide if you wish to keep those levels distinct or, instead, lump them together into one formative-assessment glob. It's totally your choice.

In the final chapter of the book, we'll deal with the real-world limitations of formative assessment, and then I'll send you off into the sunset with an epilogue, followed by a collection of resources that represents most of the important articles and books on the topic. As fair warning, many of these articles and books were written *by* academics *for* academics, and some are so stuffed with citations of other writers' work that they end up being downright difficult to read. I've indicated, with the adroit affixing of a star, those resources I regard as being especially useful to practitioners.

As I wrap up these prefatory remarks, I want to alert you to a key theme you'll encounter more than a few times in the pages ahead. Here it is: *Don't let pursuit of the instructionally perfect prevent you from reaping the rewards of the instructionally possible.*

As an enthusiastic supporter of formative assessment, I hope to convince you to join me in my boosterism. If you're a teacher, I hope you will use formative assessment in your classroom. If you're an administrator, I hope you'll encourage teachers to use formative assessment in their classrooms. But, as is true with almost any instructional intervention, it is possible to install formative assessment procedures that are too elaborate and too time consuming. Instructional interventions like those rarely survive for long; in their "perfection," they become aversive and likely to be abandoned. Better by far to adopt less perfect but more palatable approaches. Students who routinely experience the classroom benefits of less-than-perfect formative assessment will be better off educationally than will students whose teachers have discarded formative assessment because "it's too darn much work."

When, in April 2007, I spoke with representatives of the Association for Supervision and Curriculum Development (ASCD) about doing this book, we concurred that there was not only enormous interest in formative assessment throughout the community of educators but also wide-ranging confusion about what formative assessment actually is. Accordingly, when I signed up to write the book, I agreed to "really haul" so that Auntie ASCD could get the book out to the field as soon as possible and perhaps head off some misuse of this potentially powerful instructional approach. I appreciate the efforts of ASCD's superlative editors (Katie Martin's editorial ministrations were, in a word, magnificent) and production staff to get the book into print and into educators' hands in a hurry. As usual, I am in debt to my friend and word processor nonpareil, Dolly Bulquerin, for hustling right along with me. Because I was hurrying, my typically opaque handwriting was even sloppier than usual. Dolly's decryption skills were especially insightful. They had to be!

WJP

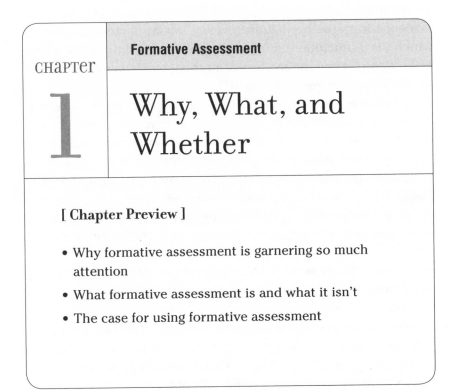

CHAPTER

1

Formative Assessment

Why, What, and Whether

[Chapter Preview]

- Why formative assessment is garnering so much attention
- What formative assessment is and what it isn't
- The case for using formative assessment

FORMATIVE ASSESSMENT WORKS! THIS PHRASE, OR SOME paraphrased version of it, is voiced with increasing frequency in many parts of the world. But *why* are more and more of today's educators touting the instructional virtues of formative assessment?

Most observers credit British researchers Paul Black and Dylan Wiliam with kicking off today's worldwide interest in formative assessment. In 1998, Black and Wiliam published two important works: an article in the journal *Phi Delta Kappan* and an extensive review of empirical research studies focused on classroom assessment. In their *Kappan* article, Black and Wiliam

(1998b) argue that formative assessment, properly employed in the classroom, will help students learn what is being taught to a substantially better degree. They support this argument with evidence from their research review (1998a), a meta-analysis in which they conclude that student gains in learning triggered by formative assessment are "amongst the largest ever reported for educational interventions" (p. 61).

Once educators realized there was ample evidence that formative assessment really was an effective way to improve student learning, it wasn't long before they began investigating the implications and asking the all too obvious follow-up question: If formative assessment could improve student learning in the classroom, couldn't it *also* improve student test scores on external accountability tests? Considering that so many educators are now figuratively drowning in an ocean of accountability, it's not surprising to see formative assessment cast in the role of life preserver. If it is true that drowning people will grasp at straws in an effort to stay afloat, it is surely as true that they will grasp even more eagerly at "research-proven" straws.

This is not to suggest that all advocates of formative assessment see it primarily as a strategy to fend off pervasive accountability pressure. Many believe that formative assessment will simply help educators do a better job of teaching. These educators might even point out that Black and Wiliam's research synthesis focuses primarily on the classroom dividends of formative assessment and devotes little attention to its potential role in raising external test scores. And many more, if not most, formative assessment proponents choose neither camp exclusively. They believe it can have a positive effect on both students' in-class learning and students' subsequent performance on accountability tests.

All right, that's the *why* underlying today's ever-expanding interest in formative assessment. Now it's time to take a close look at the *what*: What formative assessment actually is and what it isn't.

What Is Formative Assessment?

Because there has been so much attention lavished on formative assessment lately, most of today's teachers and administrators have at least a rough idea of what it is. If you asked them to explain it, they might tell you it involves testing students in the midst of an ongoing instructional sequence and then using the test results to improve instruction. By and large, this explanation is correct.

But a "by and large correct" explanation just isn't good enough when it comes to formative assessment. As you'll see in later pages, formative assessment is a potentially transformative instructional tool that, if clearly understood and adroitly employed, can benefit both educators and their students. Mushy, "by and large correct" understandings of formative assessment will rarely allow the fullness of this assessment-based process to flower. That's why I'm now asking you to join me as I dig for a while into the innards of formative assessment.

Historical and Etymological Underpinnings

There is no single officially sanctioned and universally accepted definition of formative assessment. Educators have drawn our use of the term *formative* from Michael Scriven's (1967) ground-breaking essay about educational evaluation, in which he contrasts *summative evaluation* with *formative evaluation*. According to Scriven, if the quality of an early-version educational program is evaluated while the program is still malleable—capable of being improved because of an evaluation's results—this constitutes *formative* evaluation. In contrast, when a mature, final-version educational program is evaluated in order to make a decision about its continuation or termination, this constitutes *summative* evaluation.

Scriven's insightful split of two program-evaluation roles was widely and rapidly accepted by educational evaluators. Although a handful of early writers, notably Bloom (1969), attempted to transplant the formative/summative *evaluation* distinction directly onto *assessment*, few educators were interested in investigating this idea further because it seemed to possess few practical implications for the day-to-day world of schooling.

In fact, it was only during the past decade or two that educators began to discuss whether a distinction between the formative and summative roles of assessment could benefit teachers' instructional decisions. When meaningful interest in this assessment difference finally blossomed, the essence of Scriven's original distinction between the two roles of educational evaluation was retained. That is, we continue to see formative assessment as a way to improve the caliber of still-underway instructional activities and summative assessment as a way to determine the effectiveness of already-completed instructional activities.

With these origins understood, it's time to press on toward the definition of formative assessment that we'll use in this book.

A Carefully Considered Definition

The Council of Chief State School Officers (CCSSO) is a major U.S. organization composed of individuals who head the educational system of each state. These officials, typically referred to as "state superintendents" or "state commissioners," are either elected by popular vote or appointed by governors or state boards of education. The "chiefs" have enormous educational influence in their respective states, and in 2006, when CCSSO launched a major initiative focused on a more balanced use of educational assessment and a heightened emphasis on formative assessment, it was a significant policy shift likely to have long-lasting influence on practices in U.S. public schools.

A central activity in the CCSSO assessment initiative was the creation of a new consortium focused specifically on formative assessment. A CCSSO consortium is composed of key department of education personnel from those states that wish to participate. Each of these groups is referred to as a State Collaborative on Assessment and Student Standards (SCASS), and a new SCASS dealing exclusively with formative assessment, known as Formative Assessment for Students and Teachers—or FAST SCASS, if you're in a hurry—was formed in mid-2006.

FAST SCASS held its inaugural meeting in Austin, Texas, in October 2006, with about 60 participants representing roughly 25 states. The chief mission of the four-day meeting was to reach consensus on a definition of formative assessment, with the ultimate aim of shaping the way U.S. educators understand this practice. Prominent among the concerns of the FAST SCASS members was that the definition reflect the latest research findings regarding assessment practices found to improve the quality of students' learning. Remember this point. It is important.

After considering a variety of earlier definitions, and after numerous foreseeable rounds of participants' wordsmithing, the FAST SCASS group adopted the following definition:

> Formative assessment is a process used by teachers and students during instruction that provides feedback to adjust ongoing teaching and learning to improve students' achievement of intended instructional outcomes.

Let's look at the key features of the FAST SCASS definition:

- Formative assessment is a *process*, not any particular test.
- It is used not just by teachers but by *both teachers and students*.
- Formative assessment takes place *during instruction*.
- It provides *assessment-based feedback* to teachers and students.
- The function of this feedback is to help teachers and students make *adjustments* that will improve students' achievement of intended curricular aims.

I took part in those October 2006 deliberations, and I was relatively pleased with the group's final definition and delighted that it was adopted without dissent. I sincerely hope the FAST SCASS definition will be widely used. But we're not going to use that definition in *this* book. Frankly, I believe that in our effort to scrupulously reflect the research findings available to us and satisfy the definitional preferences of all the meeting participants, our FAST SCASS group produced a definition that is verbally cumbersome. Although I have no quarrel with what the definition says, it just doesn't say it succinctly enough.

A More Succinct and Useful Definition

What educators really need is a definition of formative assessment that helps them instantly recognize what's most important about this approach. Thus, with apologies to my FAST SCASS colleagues, I present *my* definition of formative assessment, the one we'll be using in this book:

> Formative assessment is a planned process in which assessment-elicited evidence of students' status is used by teachers to adjust their ongoing instructional procedures or by students to adjust their current learning tactics.

As is typical of progeny, the above conceptualization of formative assessment shares much with the FAST SCASS definition from whence it came:

• Again, formative assessment is not a test but a process—a *planned* process involving a number of different activities.

• One of those activities is the *use of assessments*, both formal and informal, to elicit *evidence regarding students' status*: the degree to which a particular student has mastered a particular skill or body of knowledge.

• Based on this evidence, *teachers adjust* their ongoing instructional activities or *students adjust* the procedures they're currently using to try to learn whatever they're trying to learn.

Phrasing it more tersely still:

> Formative assessment is a planned process in which teachers or students use assessment-based evidence to adjust what they're currently doing.

Now, let's take a slightly deeper look at each of the key attributes of this conception of formative assessment.

A planned process. Formative assessment involves a series of carefully considered, distinguishable acts on the part of teachers *or* students *or* both. Some of those acts involve educational assessments, but the assessments play a role in the process—they are not the process itself. An educator who refers to "*a* formative test" has not quite grasped the concept, because there's no such thing. There are tests that can be used as part of the multistep, formative assessment process, but each of those tests is only a part of the process.

If you accept the distinction between the formative and summative use of test results, then you will recognize that students' results on a particular test might be used for either a summative or a formative purpose. It is not the *nature* of the test that earns the label formative or summative but the *use* to which that test's results will be put. If the purpose of Test *X* is to provide teachers and students with the evidence they need to make any warranted adjustments, then Test *X* is playing a role in the formative assessment process.

Assessment-elicited evidence. The adjustment decisions teachers and students make during the formative assessment process must be based not on whim but on evidence of the students' current level of mastery with respect to certain skills or bodies of knowledge. Accordingly, the assessment procedures designed to generate this evidence are an indispensable element of the process. Although teachers may certainly employ paper-and-pencil tests for this purpose, they can also obtain the evidence they need via a wide variety of less traditional and much less formal assessment ploys, many of which I will describe later in this book.

Teachers' instructional adjustments. Formative assessment's raison d'être is to improve students' learning. One of the most obvious ways to do this is for teachers to improve how they're teaching. Accordingly, one component of the formative assessment process is for teachers to adjust their ongoing instructional activities. Relying on assessment-based evidence of students' current status, such as test results showing that students are weak in their mastery of a particular cognitive skill, a teacher might decide to provide additional or different instruction related to this skill.

It's worth stressing that because the formative assessment process deals with *ongoing* instruction, any teacher-made modifications in instructional activities must focus on students' mastery of the curricular aims *currently* being pursued. It's not a matter of looking at test data and deciding to try a new approach next time; it's a matter of doing something different (or differently) *now*.

Students' learning tactic adjustments. Within the formative assessment process, students also take a look at assessment evidence and, if need be, make changes in how they're trying to learn. Consider, for example, a high school student who is working toward becoming a better public speaker by practicing a particular speech many times before a mirror. That repeated, solo-mirror practice is the student's learning tactic; based on assessment evidence, this tactic may or may not need adjustment.

I want to wrap up this definition overview by circling back to something very important. One of the most difficult tasks for educators who accept this conception of formative assessment is to grasp the overarching idea that it is a process rather than a test. You may have noted that in many of the preceding paragraphs I have referred to the "formative assessment process." That triple-word phrasing was a ploy to drive the point home. From here on, whenever you see the phrase *formative assessment*, I trust you'll know that it refers to a multistep process and not to a particular assessment tool.

Why We Need Definitional Clarity

Why have I been making such a fuss about a definition of formative assessment? Is it just so you won't talk past your colleagues when you discuss formative assessment with them? No, there's a more important reason, and it stems from what we do know about certain applications of educational assessment and what we don't know about others.

There are certain educational assessment practices that empirical evidence has shown to have a positive influence on student learning. There are other educational assessment practices that research has not (or has not yet) shown to have this effect. Educators need to be able to distinguish between the former and the latter. Why? So that they will be forearmed against commercial test-development companies that are eager to hitch a profit-making ride on the enthusiasm for formative assessment and, thus, will label as "formative assessment" practices that *are not actually consonant with the body of research that validates formative assessment* and, therefore, may not deliver the instructional benefits accompanying appropriately implemented formative assessment.

To illustrate how easily educators might be led astray, we need only consider the number of testing companies that are distributing as "formative assessments" products typically referred to as *interim* or *benchmark* tests. An interim or benchmark test is one that is administered periodically (perhaps once every two or three months) to measure students' status with respect to mastery of important curricular outcomes. An example of such outcomes might be 15 state-identified mathematical skills assessed each May by a statewide accountability test. A commercial test vendor might develop three different forms of an "interim test" to assess these skills. With each form containing 75 items (5 items per state-identified math skill), the test is designed to provide an indication of a student's mastery status with respect to all 15 skills. The test vendor's marketing materials might suggest that teachers administer the forms at various intervals during the school year: perhaps Form 1 in the fall, Form 2 just after winter break, and Form 3 in the spring, one month before the date of the statewide accountability test. The test vendor would send teachers the results of the interim tests, thus providing 3 snapshots of their students' current status in regard to the 15 state-sanctioned mathematics skills that will be measured "for keeps" in May.

This sort of periodic assessment may be a good thing to do. It may help teachers do a better instructional job with their students by, for example, helping teachers accurately predict which of their students are likely to have difficulty with the May math accountability test and go on to single-out those students for particular attention. *But there is currently no research evidence supporting the hypothesis that this kind of periodic assessment is educationally beneficial.* Thus, describing interim or benchmark tests as "formative" in the sense that they are in accord with research evidence such as that synthesized by Black and Wiliam (1998a) is a fundamental misrepresentation. A test vendor touting them as such is being disingenuous or, as we used to say, is *lying*.

It is not only profit-preoccupied commercial vendors who mislabel their assessments as formative. In more than a few states and school districts, educators have created periodically administered assessments that they characterize as "formative" and go on to disseminate with great enthusiasm. One suspects that these educators, in a well-meant effort to assist classroom teachers, have tried to develop periodic assessments that will be instructionally beneficial. And perhaps those assessments *will* help teachers. But again, *there is no evidence that these district-developed or state-developed assessments boost student achievement.* Characterizing these periodic tests as "formative" is simply inaccurate. I'm not suggesting that district- or state-level educators are affixing the label to their tests for nefarious purposes; they're simply being imprecise about their conceptualization of what formative assessment truly is.

And *that's* why I have lavished so much attention on a defensible definition of formative assessment—one reflecting the key attributes of formative assessment that empirical research evidence has shown to improve student learning. The future may yet yield evidence that alternative assessment approaches are similarly effective. But for the time being, the closer your "formative assessment" practices and procedures match my definition, the more likely it is they will deliver the instructional benefits you desire. It's the difference between *very probably* getting a return on your investment and *maybe just possibly* getting one. If I were a teacher, I know the choice I would make.

Is Formative Assessment Always Classroom Assessment?

We've just about concluded our definitional digging, but there's one more important issue that still needs to be addressed. Put simply, as formative assessment is defined in this book, does it necessarily need to be *classroom* assessment? Is it possible, say, for *administrators* in states, districts, or schools to install and operate the sort of assessment-rooted process envisioned in the definition we've been dissecting, or must that kind of process spring exclusively from the activities of a particular teacher in a particular classroom?

Well, we know for sure that all *classroom* assessment need not be *formative* assessment. That's because teachers could administer frequent tests with the exclusive purpose of assigning grades and not try at all to use data from such tests to improve instruction. But the question under consideration is a little different: Must formative assessment, by its very nature, take place only at the classroom level?

You can arrive at your own judgment about this issue, but let me get my own answer on the table so you'll at least recognize my preference. Although it might be technically possible to encounter versions of formative assessment that have been externally imposed on classrooms rather than emerging from those classrooms themselves, this would be really rare. It should be. Formative assessment that really pays off for students will, I believe, be *classroom* formative assessment.

Remember, for formative assessment (as we define it) to exist at all, it must lead to instructional adjustment decisions by teachers or learning tactic adjustment decisions by students, and these adjustments will affect activities or efforts already in progress. The decisions to adjust or not to adjust, and the decisions about the nature of any adjustments (the *what* and the *how*) need to be made on the spot or almost on the spot—when there's still instructional and learning time available. It's because of this limited time frame that when I think of formative assessment, I always precede it with an invisible modifier. Formative assessment, to me, is *classroom* formative assessment.

Figure 1.1 shows illustrative proportions of formative assessment that might be seen in many classrooms. The classrooms at
the far left are those in which all assessment is grading focused
rather than improvement focused. These are classrooms where
there is plenty of classroom assessment but zero formative
assessment. The classrooms at the far right are those in which
almost all classroom assessment, both formal and informal, has
a formative improvement mission. The middle two circles represent token or moderate uses of formative assessments as part of
a teacher's classroom assessment activities. The two circles at
the extreme right are not completely coterminous (one of my
favorite words, meaning "having identical borders") because, in
most settings, there will be some required minimum of classroom assessment activities that must be devoted to the determination of students' grades.

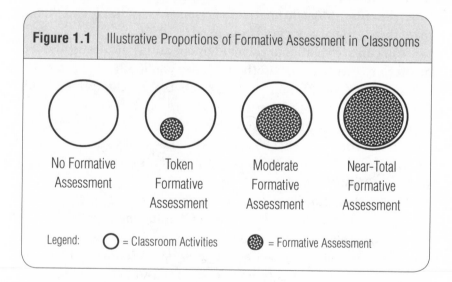

Figure 1.1 | Illustrative Proportions of Formative Assessment in Classrooms

No Formative Assessment   Token Formative Assessment   Moderate Formative Assessment   Near-Total Formative Assessment

Legend: ◯ = Classroom Activities   ⬤ = Formative Assessment

Whether to Use Formative Assessment

We've looked briefly at the *why* (why there's so much fuss about
formative assessment these days), and we've also taken a pretty
thorough look at the *what* (what the meaning of formative assessment is). Now we need to consider the *whether*, namely, whether

teachers ought to employ formative assessment in their own classrooms.

For educators, now is when this book gets personal. We are no longer talking in the abstract about definitions or the reasons other folks have been focusing on formative assessment. If you're a teacher, the time has come to start wrestling with the vital question of whether formative assessment is something you ought to do, for your own sake and for the sake of your students. If you're an administrator, it's time to begin tussling with the issue of whether you will advocate formative assessment among those teachers with whom you work.

There are essentially two ways educators arrive at decisions about whether to alter the way they approach instruction: (1) by accepting a data-free argument that a new approach is worthwhile and (2) by accepting the research-based evidence of a new approach's efficacy. Let's consider each.

A Data-Free Argument

Many educators choose to implement or advocate new instructional approaches simply because they've been persuaded by the well-articulated positions of advocates. Given that there is a ton of artistry in teaching, trying out a new method because someone speaks highly of it is a perfectly reasonable way for teachers to tinker with their instructional approaches. You show me a teacher who hasn't tried out an instructional tactic based on someone else's recommendation, and I'll show you a teacher who is rooted in rigidity. If someone puts forward what seems to be a smart way of improving instruction, it often makes sense to take that idea out for a spin in your own classes.

If you're looking for an advocate of formative assessment, clearly you've come to the right place. Given the topic of this book, it shouldn't surprise you that I am one. I believe that *all* teachers should use this process because, when it's properly implemented, formative assessment will improve how well students learn. Moreover, because evidence of improved student learning is likely to be regarded as evidence of a teacher's own instructional effectiveness, formative assessment has the happy effect of helping successful teachers be accurately regarded as successful.

Here's the thrust of my evidence-free argument in favor of formative assessment. First off, teachers function in order to help kids learn, but few teachers will always create perfect instructional designs the first time around. Most discover that even their best-laid instructional plans usually need to be massaged, sometimes meaningfully, in order to work optimally. And if this is so, then why not make such massaging as potent as possible by finding out about students' current status during an ongoing instructional process? It makes eminent sense for teachers to alter their instructional procedures only after getting an accurate fix on their students' current achievement status. It makes eminent sense for teachers to provide students with the assessment-based evidence those students will need when deciding how well their learning tactics are working. In short, it makes eminent sense to rely on assessment-based evidence about students' skills and knowledge before figuring out how to help those students learn better.

Instruction should not be a Ouija-boardlike game in which teachers guess about what to do next. Educating kids is far too important for that sort of approach. Rather, instructing students should be a carefully conceived enterprise in which decisions about what to do next are predicated on the best available information. And the best available information about what to do next almost always flows from a determination about what students currently know and can do. Formative assessment supplies the evidence a teacher needs in order to make any necessary instructional adjustments. Formative assessment supplies the evidence students need in order to make any necessary adjustments in how they are trying to learn something. Formative assessment, then, can help both teachers teach better and learners learn better.

So, even if there were not a shred of empirical evidence to support the worth of formative assessment in the classroom, I would still be advocating its use because it makes so darn much sense! Thus, the first reason I hope you will adopt formative assessment in your own classroom or advocate its adoption in other classrooms is because formative assessment constitutes the key cornerstone of clearheaded instructional thinking. Formative assessment represents *evidence-based* instructional decision making. If you want to become more instructionally effective, and if you want your students to achieve more, then formative assessment should be for you.

An Evidence-Based Case

Of course, teachers' other approach to coming up with improved ways to teach their students is to adopt *research-proven* instructional procedures. Because the advocacy of formative assessment you'll find in this book rests chiefly on this second approach, it is important for you to understand both the strengths and shortcomings of "research-proven" instructional strategies.

Having research evidence on your side is wonderful; in the midst of a disagreement, all you need to do is choose the right moment to roll out your research evidence and, if the evidence is sufficiently compelling, you'll be running up the victory flag in a matter of minutes. Unfortunately, when professionals in the field of education assert that a procedure is "research proven," we typically mean something different from what professionals in many other fields mean when they invoke this description. Let's consider why.

Proof and probability. Educational research revolves around human beings, most of whom are *little* human beings. And human beings, regardless of their size, are complicated creatures. As a consequence, even if we rely on results of research studies simply reeking of methodological rigor, *rarely* can we say that "if a teacher takes Action *X*, then the teacher's students will unquestionably end up achieving Outcome *Z*." Education, because it involves human beings, is just too complex. Every instructional situation involves a *particular* teacher whose unique background makes that teacher profoundly different from a teacher born on the very same day in the same hospital and raised just down the street by a pair of equally loving parents. Teachers themselves are a widely divergent variable, whether it is because of DNA dif-ferences or because of their idiosyncratic experiences. *Particular* teachers also function in settings where there are *particular* prin-cipals, *particular* colleagues, and, most important of all, *particular* kids. Teaching, in short, is such a particularistic endeavor that, with remarkably few exceptions, the best we can ever derive from educational research investigations is *probability-based* instructional guidance.

What this means is that even if several education research studies arrive at essentially identical findings, the most apt con-clusion a teacher can draw from such findings will be something along these lines: "If I engage in this research-supported instruc-tional action, it is *likely* that my students will learn what I want them to learn." Even the most compelling of "research-proven" conclusions typically can't go much beyond something such as, "If you do this thing, it is *probable* that you'll get the result you want."

Yes, the patent particularism of real-world instruction always requires us to regard "research proven" as providing probabilis-tic guidance rather than as supplying us with definitive truths. However, let's not knock probabilistic guidance. If profes-sionals—be they surgeons, attorneys, or teachers—can increase their odds of achieving a desired result even slightly, those pro-fessionals should always opt for the improved-probability course of action. Just ask any professional gambler about the dividends of having the odds "ever so slightly" on your side.

Examining the evidence. Clearly, we need to look at the evi-dence supporting the dividends of formative assessment. Just how compelling is that evidence? If you are a teacher, is it sufficiently compelling for you to personally install formative assessment as an integral part of your own approach to instruc-tion? If you are an administrator, is it sufficiently compelling for you to personally urge your teacher-colleagues to incorporate formative assessment as an integral part of their own classroom instruction?

As indicated earlier, much of the current interest in formative assessment, especially in the United States and Canada, was spurred by the work of two British researchers, Paul Black and Dylan Wiliam. Their *Kappan* essay (1998b) draws heavily on their own extensive *meta-analysis* of classroom formative assessment published earlier the same year in a special issue of the journal *Assessment in Education* (1998a). In that synthesis of research studies, Black and Wiliam conclude that "the research reported here shows conclusively that formative assessment does improve learning" (1998a, p. 49).

These days, one often encounters advocates of certain instructional interventions who support their advocacy by invoking meta-analyses as though a meta-analysis report constitutes some sort of sanctified scripture. Meta-analyses are not holy writ. They differ dramatically in quality simply because analysis is an endeavor requiring judgment. The work of a meta-analyst requires many along-the-way judgments. If all of those judgments are defensible, then we can place reasonable confidence in the conclusions of the meta-analysis. If some of those judgments are indefensible, then confidence quickly crumbles.

Thus, you should not routinely defer to the array of numerical effect sizes that often seems to conclude a meta-analysis in a quantitative (hence "credible") manner. Those numbers bubble forth from a judgmental stew of the meta-analyst's own making. *The confidence you should place in the conclusions of a meta-analysis should be completely dependent on the caliber of the meta-analysis itself.* And this brings us directly to the specific meta-analysis that has galvanized educators' interest in formative assessment.

The Black and Wiliam meta-analysis. "Assessment and Classroom Learning" (Black & Wiliam, 1998a) was published in the journal *Assessment in Education* along with comments on the analysis by leading educational experts from several nations. Let's consider, then, the essential features of the Black and Wiliam meta-analysis.

They based it on nine years' worth of research reports and used two earlier extensive reviews (Crooks, 1988; Natriello, 1987) as starting points. Focusing on formative classroom assessment defined essentially in the same manner as it has been defined in

META-ANALYSIS: MAKING SENSE OF THE MYRIAD

Serious educational research has been under way in the United States for more than a century, and the volume of that research seems to be expanding at an almost exponential rate. Consider that in 1958, when I made my first trip to the annual meeting of the American Educational Research Association (AERA), the total attendance was about 300. Approximately 200 research papers were submitted for presentation, and 100 papers were presented. Fifty years later, in 2007, almost 16,000 researchers attended the AERA Annual Meeting, more than 10,000 research papers were submitted, and about 3,000 papers were presented. More research is a good thing, of course, but beyond a certain point, the volume of it can be overwhelming. Back in 1958, I might have been able to read *all* the 100 research reports presented at that year's AERA meeting over the span of a weekend. There is no way I or anyone could have read every report presented at the 2007 meeting over a weekend—not even a three-day weekend! If a relevant research report falls outside the range of an interested educator's reading-volume capacity, does it still make a sound?

It does now. Insightful researchers, recognizing that there are too few three-day weekends and far too many research reports to make sense of, provided a solution: *meta-analysis*. The leader of this effort was Gene Glass of Arizona State University, who not only pioneered the method of meta-analysis but provided readily understood quantitative tactics for coalescing the results of dis-similar investigations. The Greek prefix, *meta*, means "beyond," signifying that meta-analysts aim to carry out analyses *beyond* the individual study results under review. Skilled meta-analysts can synthesize the results from a variety of studies so that, despite study-to-study differences, we can still derive generalizable con-clusions from a welter of seemingly divergent investigations. With good reason, meta-analysis has become a powerful tool to help educators comprehend the huge array of research now available.

this book, Black and Wiliam were able to identify 681 publications that appeared potentially relevant to their review. From those 681 contenders, they read approximately 250 reports in full and used them in the final meta-analysis. You can find a detailed description of the procedures employed in the identification and scrutiny of possible publications in the report of the Black and Wiliam meta-analysis (1998a). The studies they considered were diverse in nature: carried out by researchers in several nations, involving students ranging from 5-year-olds to undergraduates, and focused on a variety of subject fields. Although classroom formative assessment was an explicit focus of many of the studies included in the meta-analysis, in some instances the use of formative assessment was only ancillary to a particular study's chief investigative focus.

Based on their meta-analysis, Black and Wiliam report typical effect sizes of between 0.4 and 0.7 in favor of students taught in classrooms where formative assessment was employed. Such effect sizes, the two meta-analysts observe, "are larger than most of those found for educational interventions" (1998b, p. 141). To help their readers understand the meaning of such effect sizes, Black and Wiliam point out that an effect-size gain of 0.7 in a recent 41-nation international study of mathematics would have raised the rank of a middle-of-the-pack country to one of the top-5 nations. A particularly important finding in the bulk of the meta-analyzed studies is that "improved formative assessment helps low achievers more than other students—and so reduces the range of achievement while raising achievement overall" (Black & Wiliam, 1998b, p. 141).

In their lengthy report of this meta-analysis, Black and Wiliam are also particularly attentive to the considerable variety of studies with which they were working. Nonetheless, their overall conclusion is strikingly supportive of the contribution that formative assessment can make to the instructional process:

> The consistent feature across the variety of these examples is that they all show that attention to formative assessment can lead to significant learning gains. Although there is no guarantee that it will do

so irrespective of the particular approach adopted, we have not come across any report of negative effects following an enhancement of formative practice. (1998a, p. 17)

The absence of reported negative effects linked to formative assessment is worth noting, for in many meta-analyses of instructional interventions, the meta-analysts discover a number of results representing either "no significant differences" or differences actually favoring the "untreated" students.

Black and Wiliam emphasize that they have not offered "optimal modes" to follow in the installation of classroom formative assessment. Happily, as these two researchers point out,

the range of conditions and contexts under which studies have shown that gains can be achieved must indicate that the principles that underlie achievement of substantial improvements in learning are robust. Significant gains can be achieved by many different routes, and initiatives here are not likely to fail through neglect of delicate and subtle features. (1998a, p. 61)

This is reassuring. However, Black and Wiliam wrap up their extensive review with a powerful caution to practitioners, namely, that "the changes in classroom practice are central rather than marginal, and have to be incorporated by each teacher into his or her practice in his or her own way" (1998a, p. 62).

When considering the persuasiveness of a meta-analysis, the confidence we should ascribe to it must be derived from the quality with which that analysis was carried out. Most reviewers of the Black and Wiliam meta-analysis conclude that both the caliber of methodological rigor employed and the high quality of the judgments used throughout render this important review worthy of our confidence. The overwhelmingly positive results found in almost a decade's worth of diverse empirical investigations lends powerful support to the notion that "formative assessment works!" Accordingly, if you're a teacher, you ought to make it work for your students' well-being. And if you're an administrator who supports teachers' efforts, you ought to advocate formative assessment's adoption.

The Effectiveness Issue

Teachers, especially seasoned ones, know from bitter experience that there's a decisive difference between (1) an instructional procedure and (2) an *effective* instructional procedure. So far in this chapter, we've considered *why* there's so much interest in formative assessment, *what* formative assessment is, and *whether* teachers ought to employ formative assessment in their own classrooms.

You'll notice, however, that we have not focused on distinguishing between formative assessment that's flawed and formative assessment that's fabulous. Please be patient. Later on, we'll get to the important issue of how to maximize formative assessment's quality, but to tackle the quality issue sensibly, it will be necessary to do so in a particular way. If you had an opportunity to read the preface to this book (and if you actually did read it), you saw that we'll be looking at four distinctive levels of formative assessment. Well, it simply makes more sense to deal with *per-level* quality factors rather than pretending one set of quality considerations will apply to all four strikingly different levels.

If at this point you have acquired a reasonably solid undertaking of what formative assessment is, I promise, by the end of the book you'll have an equally solid understanding of how to estimate the likelihood that a given implementation of formative assessment will work well.

SUPER-SUCCINCT SUMMARY

- Formative assessment is a planned process in which assessment-elicited evidence of students' status is used by teachers to adjust their ongoing instructional procedures or by students to adjust their current learning tactics.

- Because formative assessment has been shown to improve students' in-class learning, many educators have adopted it in the hope that it will also raise their students' performances on accountability tests.

- The expanded use of formative assessment is supported not only by instructional logic but also by the conclusions of a well-conceived and skillfully implemented meta-analysis by Paul Black and Dylan Wiliam.

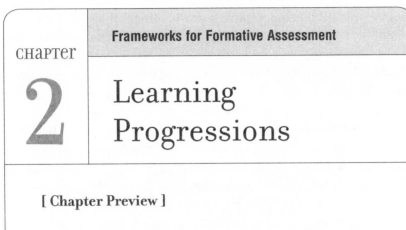

2

Frameworks for Formative Assessment

Learning Progressions

[**Chapter Preview**]

- What a learning progression is and what it isn't
- Why learning progressions are integral to formative assessment
- How to build a learning progression
- What a finished learning progression looks like

FORMATIVE ASSESSMENT IS ALL ABOUT DECISION MAKING. Those decisions, made by both teachers and students, invariably revolve around the following two-part question: "Is an adjustment needed, and, if so, what should that adjustment be?"

When teachers answer this two-part query, they're typically focusing on whether they need to adjust ongoing or upcoming instructional activities—what they're doing in class and what they're having their students do. When students answer this same two-parter, they're focusing on whether they need to adjust their learning tactics—the techniques they're using as they try to learn something. The distinctive feature of the *adjustment*

decisions made during formative assessment is that those decisions are determined chiefly by *assessment-elicited evidence* of
students' current skills or knowledge. OK, so much for generali-
ties. Now it's time to get more specific about what to assess and
when in the formative assessment process the adjustments
should be made.

Theoretically, teachers and students could make an adjustment decision in the wake of every incoming piece of assessment
information. But, in the real world, this is unrealistic and would
be exhausting for both the enervated teachers and decision-
drained students. Indeed, one of the challenges facing any
teacher who employs formative assessment is to arrive at a sensible number of assessment-informed adjustments for consideration. And that's precisely the point at which teachers need to
turn to learning progressions.

What Is a Learning Progression?

A *learning progression* is a sequenced set of subskills and bodies
of enabling knowledge that, it is believed, students must master
en route to mastering a more remote curricular aim. In other
words, it is composed of the step-by-step building blocks students are presumed to need in order to successfully attain a
more distant, designated instructional outcome. The more "distant" instructional outcome, known as the *target curricular aim*,
is typically a skill (rather than a body of knowledge) and usually
a significant skill at that—the kind of learning outcome requiring
a number of lessons for students to achieve it. An example of
such a skill in, say, science or social studies would be students'
abilities to appropriately portray complex sets of data in tables,
figures, or graphs. In mathematics, a target curricular aim might
call for students to be able to arrive at suitable solutions to real-
world word problems requiring the use of two or more mathematical operations. Although most learning progressions are
built toward high-level cognitive skills such as the examples I've
mentioned, they can also be designed to identify the building

blocks underlying the acquisition of *psychomotor* skills, for example, small-muscle skills such as keyboarding or large-muscle skills such as pole vaulting.

Within a learning progression, a body of *enabling knowledge* is a set of facts or information the student must memorize or understand. If the target curricular aim is composing a persuasive essay, for example, the enabling knowledge would include a collection of generally approved word-usage rules. A *subskill* in a learning progression is usually a cognitive skill that, though lesser in scope or importance than that called for in a target curricular aim, is regarded as necessary before a student can master that more advanced cognitive skill. Examples of subskills for essay writing would include students' ability to (1) properly organize the essay's content and (2) create an attention-arresting opening paragraph.

Finally, the historically minded among you and those inclined to read further on the topic may be interested to know that several decades ago the typical label used when describing such collections of sequenced building blocks was a *task analysis*. More recently, Australian researchers have identified these same building-block sequences as *progress maps* (Forster & Masters, 1996).

Because many educators find it easier to work with graphically portrayed learning progressions than with verbally described learning progressions, please consider Figure 2.1. In that figure you will see a set of building blocks—subskills (circles) and bodies of enabling knowledge (squares)—to be achieved by students on their way to mastering a target curricular aim (the rectangle at the top of the sequence). The five building blocks are sequenced to indicate the order in which the learning progression's designer (often a teacher) believes students should achieve them. Figure 2.1's manner of depicting a learning progression as a vertical sequence is typical of the way most learning progression are illustrated graphically, but you will sometimes see them set up horizontally, from left to right, as in Figure 2.2. One of the advantages of a horizontal representation is that it's easy to insert the projected amount of instructional time needed for each building block according to the actual dates of instruction and numbers of lessons planned.

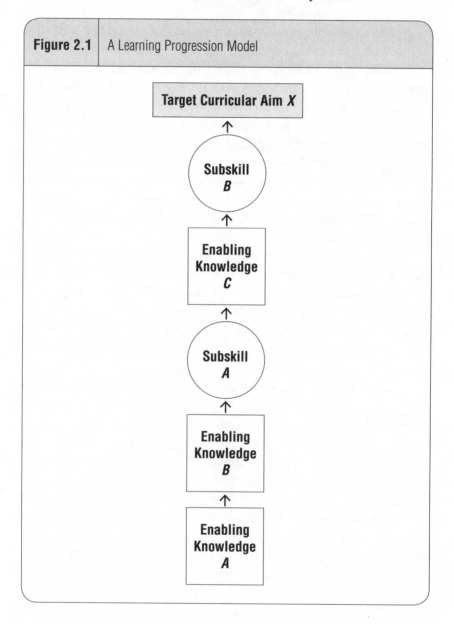

Figure 2.1 | A Learning Progression Model

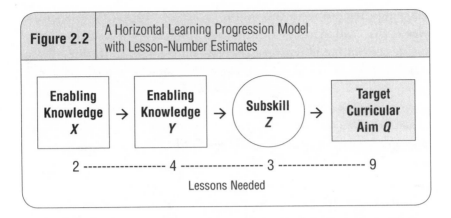

Figure 2.2 — A Horizontal Learning Progression Model with Lesson-Number Estimates

Why are learning progressions so pivotal in the successful implementation of formative assessment? They are the backdrop against which teachers and students can determine when to collect what sort of evidence regarding students' current status. They provide a framework that helps teachers identify appropriate adjustment-decision points as well as the kinds of en route assessment evidence they need.

What a Learning Progression Isn't

Before the applause for learning progressions begins to subside, let's consider what a learning progression *isn't*.

A learning progression isn't unerringly accurate. A well-conceived learning progression—its building blocks and the way those building blocks are sequenced—represents the best instructional thinking of the person or persons who created it. But that thinking may be flawed. The building blocks may not, in fact, be the right ones students need in order to attain the target curricular aim. They may not, in fact, be arranged in the best sequence to support mastery. Because learning progressions typically represent educators' best instructional thinking, and even well-intentioned instructional thinking can go haywire, learning progressions should be regarded not as flawless frameworks but, rather, as best-judgment framework *hypotheses*.

A particular learning progression isn't suitable for all students. Students differ—an insight that hardly comes as a surprise to any seasoned educator. Moreover, those differences embrace an enormous array of significant variables, not the least of which are associated with students' idiosyncratic (and sometimes vexing to teachers) learning styles. Putting it simply, different kids often learn things in strikingly different ways.

Because of sometimes profound differences in the ways individuals learn, it should be apparent that any specific learning progression is not likely to work equally well for all students. When encountering a given learning progression's building blocks, some students may be more likely to "leapfrog, then circle back" than to move in the linear sequence embodied in the learning progression's building-block order. Other students may need to learn things in much smaller increments than is required by most of their classmates. Although the learning progression represents a best-judgment hypothesis of how the greatest number of students will learn, a wise teacher accepts from the start that it can never be a "one-size-fits-all-well" sequence. Always be prepared to encounter students who may need their building blocks in a different sequence or different building blocks altogether. And never succumb to the alluring belief that your learning progression constitutes the one and only way for students to master the targeted curricular aim.

A learning progression isn't necessarily better because it's more complex. Things that are more sophisticated or complicated are often regarded as preferable to things that are unsophisticated and uncomplicated. With respect to learning progressions, such is not the case. If you run into a learning progression that has only two or three building blocks rather than a dozen such building blocks, this does not immediately signify that the bare-bones learning progression is necessarily inferior to its complex counterpart. The fundamental reality is that an *unused* learning progression can't enhance anyone's instruction.

If a learning progression is so complex that it proves off-putting to a potential user, then it's *too* complex.

We will deal with the issue of a learning progression's complexity more completely later in the chapter when we consider learning progression construction. However, now, while we're thinking about the essential nature of a learning progression, it's important to stress that there must always be a balance between (1) the level of analytic sophistication that goes into a learning progression and (2) the likelihood of the learning progression being used by teachers and students.

The Criticality of Learning Progressions

To make formative assessment function most effectively, it is almost always necessary for teachers to employ learning progressions as the frameworks by which they can identify appropriate occasions for assessment-informed adjustment decisions. Learning progressions, in an almost literal sense, become the maps that provide guidance on how best to carry out formative assessment.

Remember, formative assessment is not the occasional administration of classroom tests; it's an integral dimension of ongoing instruction whereby teachers and students adjust what they're doing. Formative assessment, therefore, becomes the chief activity through which teachers monitor how well they're teaching something and, if necessary, determine how to adjust their instruction. Similarly, formative assessment becomes the chief activity through which students monitor how well they're learning something and, if necessary, determine how to adjust their learning tactics.

Clarifying What to Assess and When to Assess It

Teachers must be judicious in deciding when and how to elicit evidence from students. And this is precisely how a properly conceptualized learning progression can save the day. Because a learning progression lays out the subskills and bodies of enabling knowledge students seem to need in order to master the target curricular aim, it helps teachers identify the most important adjustment decisions to be made while they monitor the effectiveness of their ongoing instruction.

But what should teachers assess? The answer is, those certain subskills and enabling knowledge identified in the progression as being critical to students' mastery of a target curricular aim. When should teachers assess these subskills and enabling knowledge? The answer is, before proceeding to the next building block in the progression, the mastery of which is believed to be dependent on mastery of its predecessors. The resulting evidence of students' mastery status becomes grist for adjustment decisions. These decisions might result in fairly inconsequential alterations in a particular lesson's instructional activities, or they might lead to substantial changes including reteaching something already taught, but teaching it differently; adding brand new content to the existing instructional plans; or deleting previously planned instructional activities.

One simple way for a teacher to employ a learning progression is to *mentally* double-check that students must really master each building block in the sequence in order to attain the target curricular aim. If the teacher concludes that each building block is a bona fide prerequisite to the mastery of the target curricular aim, the teacher would know that it's important to collect formal or informal evidence regarding students' status with respect to each such building block. And if, based on this double-check, the teacher decides that the building block is *not* a true requisite for curricular-aim mastery, the teacher should delete it from the learning progression. Thus, although a learning progression supplies an initial framework for formative assessment, the teacher must still carry out a good deal of judgment making. It's here that instructional artistry must bubble gently to the surface if the instruction is going to be stellar.

MADELINE'S LAMENT

During five of the last six years that I was an active faculty member in the UCLA Graduate School of Education and Information Studies, I team-taught a course with Madeline Hunter, also a faculty member at UCLA. Madeline, who is now deceased, was in my mind the most influential staff developer in American and Canadian education during the latter half of the 20th century.

Our team-taught class focused on the relationship between teaching and testing. One of the most challenging sessions in the course was the one focused on designing a learning progression, which was known at the time as a "carrying out a task analysis." Madeline and I split chief instructional responsibilities: I would cover certain topics, and she, others. When we came to the topic of task analysis, we agreed that it was a tough topic to teach—especially to grad students. Because neither of us was particularly eager to take it on, we decided to flip a coin, and Madeline lost. That meant she had to show our first batch of students how to identify a curricular goal's precursor subskills and bodies of enabling knowledge. The goal she chose was the ability to make change from a five-dollar bill, and she worked backward from this outcome to painstakingly outline everything someone would need to know to achieve this end. She did it well, but it was an enervating session for her.

Thereafter, every time we taught the course, when we were deciding who would teach what, Madeline always ended up with the task-analysis class. "After all," I told her, "you've already done it before—and you do it so well!" Grumbling just audibly, she always agreed.

The Assessment-Based Inference at Issue

When teachers use learning progressions to guide their formative assessment decisions, those teachers are invariably focused on the same sort of assessment-based inference irrespective of whether the building block involved is a subskill or a body of enabling knowledge. Put simply, the assessment-based inference deals with whether the student has already mastered the building block completely, has partially mastered it, or has not mastered it at all. Based on assessment evidence the teacher obtains for all students or for a satisfactory proportion of those students, the teacher will make an adjustment decision. If the decision is that an adjustment is necessary, the teacher will then decide *how* to alter the instruction, a subject we'll get to in Chapter 3.

Building a Learning Progression

It's now time to get into the actual construction of learning progressions. But before we do so, let me offer an important disclaimer: Given the enormous variability in the curricular aims and the variability of the magnitude and effectiveness of the instructional activities available to promote students' attainment of those curricular aims, *it is impossible to identify a single, can't-miss procedure for constructing learning progressions.*

I can't provide a cookie-cutter approach to the construction of learning progressions any more than a building contractor could provide a cookie-cutter approach to the construction of houses. So much depends on what you're trying to build and the materials you have to work with. The variety of end results sought and what's available instructionally to teachers make it impossible to lay out a single design scheme. What I can do, though, is talk about sound construction principles.

Two Key Preliminary Considerations

Before getting under way with the creation of any learning progression, you need to deal with two issues, both of which can have a serious impact on the progression you ultimately generate.

The number of building blocks. To keep a learning progression sufficiently lean so that it is likely to be used, the only building blocks to include are those for which you plan to collect assessment evidence. Some architects of learning progressions think it helpful to lay out more elaborate sequences incorporating not only to-be-assessed building blocks but also key, unassessed but to-be-taught building blocks; this can lead to the resulting progression becoming excessively complicated.

The "grain size" of the building blocks. The second issue to face before setting out to create a learning progression is the *grain-size* quandary, that is, the question of how "big" the building blocks will be. The "grain size" of a building block reflects the nature of the content it comprises. Is it small, specific, or simple, or is it large, ambiguous, or complex? A building block of enabling knowledge might range from a "small" amount of knowledge (e.g., knowing the names of the Seven Wonders of the Ancient World) to mastery of quite a large collection of content (e.g., being familiar with all 20th-century U.S. Supreme Court decisions specifically focused on public schools). Similarly, a subskill building block might be a simple, fairly low-level cognitive skill (e.g., the ability to distinguish between complete sentences and sentence fragments) or something far more demanding (e.g., the ability to conceptualize and carry out a true scientific experiment). One useful way to think about the grain size of building blocks is to focus on the amount of instructional time it will take to get students to master them. Large building blocks are those requiring substantial amounts of instructional time; small building blocks are those requiring far less instructional time.

If the target curricular aim represents a very large grain size, then the size of a learning progression's building blocks can vary more than would have been the case had the target curricular aim been narrower in its scope. Clearly, there are many ways of approaching students' mastery of mathematical problem solving, but if the teacher's objective is to have students memorize the Gettysburg Address, the course is more prescribed. Consider, for example, the grain-size options open to a teacher (let's call him Harry) who is trying to develop a new learning progression for his 10th grade English classes. Harry's overall goal is to get his students to write first-class original essays, which is a complex, "large-grain" curricular aim. One of the things Harry has noticed is that his students' writing is peppered with many mechanical errors. When designing his learning progression, he could address this by adding a single, fairly large-grain building block (mechanics), which he would teach and assess as perhaps one of three or four large-grain building blocks in the learning progression focused on essay writing. But Harry might also address this same topic by adding a series of small-grain building blocks (punctuation, capitalization, spelling, grammar, and word choice), each of which he would teach and assess separately. If so inclined, he could make the grain sizes smaller still by subdividing punctuation into commas, semicolons, and colons—again, each of which he would teach and assess separately. If Harry chooses these smallest grain sizes, he's likely to wind up with a learning progression of a dozen or more building blocks. As a general rule of thumb, the smaller the grain size of the building blocks in a learning progression, the greater the number of building blocks the learning progression will contain.

The curricular aim's grain size is not the only factor to consider. In truth, the grain size of a learning progression's building blocks ought to be influenced most powerfully by the detail tolerance of the teacher involved. If you're a teacher who really revels in a complex series of fine-grained subskills and bodies of enabling knowledge and is likely to feel cheated if a number of such building blocks are masked by large-scope descriptors, then small-scope grain sizes are probably the ticket for you. If, however, you prefer to work with just a few building blocks— more like three or four than eight or nine—then large-scope grain sizes will likely suit you fine. In short, there is no "perfect" solution to the grain-size riddle for learning progressions. As with so many things in education, it depends. In this instance, it depends chiefly on a teacher's detail-level preferences.

What's paramount in this regard is that the learning progression is used. As you prepare to create a new learning progression, try to ascertain the tolerance-for-detail of the teacher or teachers who will be using it. If you're designing a learning progression for yourself, you'll know what to do. If you're designing for others, cleave as closely as possible to those teachers' preferences.

A Sound Construction Process

An educator attempting to construct a learning progression faces some fundamental choices. To make my description of those choices easier to follow, I'm going to set it forth in the form of specific steps. Although the four steps I recommend are in a logical order, there is nothing sacrosanct about their sequence. Seasoned developers of learning progressions may find it necessary to depart from the linear pattern represented in the four-step sequence depicted here. Finally, so that this four-step approach is more readily describable, I'm going to ask you to assume that *you* are the person who is constructing a learning progression.

Step 1. Acquire a thorough understanding of the target curricular aim. The function of a learning progression is, fundamentally, to increase the likelihood that students will master the target curricular aim. Clearly, then, you must be completely conversant with the nature of the curricular aim in question. If you have anything less than a lucid understanding of what that target curricular aim represents, it is almost certain that any learning progression you build will be less effective than you would like it to be.

How do you "thoroughly understand" a curricular aim? This is a tough question to answer, because the mere act of looking at a curricular aim, even for a long time and with rapt attention, might not be sufficiently clarifying. Here, however, are two suggestions to help you get a better grasp of what's actually involved in the target curricular aim for which you're hoping to build a learning progression.

First, try to think of *behavior-difference situations*, that is, settings in which individuals would behave differently depending on whether they *have or haven't* already mastered the target curricular aim under consideration. For example, let's assume the target curricular aim is a mathematical skill requiring students to be able to compute the area of various geometric shapes that might be encountered in the real world. Think of situations in which a "skill possessor" would behave differently than a "skill nonpossessor." For instance, if faced with calculating how much carpet would be needed to cover the floor area in three rooms of an apartment, the skill possessor should be able to identify the correct amount of carpet required; the skill nonpossessor would probably end up with too much or too little carpet. Identifying similar behavior-difference situations will usually prove helpful in promoting a solid familiarity on your part with the nature of a particular skill.

A second remarkably helpful way of clarifying the nature of a target curricular aim is to *decide on the assessment procedure or procedures you'll employ to determine whether students have mastered it.* As a practical matter, most teachers rely on only one assessment technique to verify students' end-of-instruction status with respect to a particular curricular aim, but if you have more than one assessment procedure in mind, this will usually help you get an even better fix on the nature of the target curricular aim. And please remember that these assessment methods do not have to resemble traditional paper-and-pencil tests; less formal ways of eliciting assessment evidence are often quite serviceable.

By spelling out your intended assessment approach or approaches for measuring students' curricular-aim mastery in advance, you will have "operationalized" the curricular aim itself. In other words, you will have asserted that if students perform well enough on the assessment approach you've chosen, then this "operation" will serve as a suitable surrogate for students' mastery of the aim itself. For example, if you see that your students can solve a half-dozen varied "real world" area-calculation problems, you will logically infer that they have mastered the mathematical skill on which these problems are based. Few techniques for clarifying the nature of a curricular aim are as potent as deciding in glittering detail how to measure students' status with regard to the curricular aim.

Now that you have a basic understanding of what it means to achieve a thorough understanding of the target curricular aim, let's turn to the second step in your exciting journey through the Land of Learning Progressions.

Step 2. Identify all requisite precursory subskills and bodies of enabling knowledge. The second step in building a learning progression calls for the use of crackerjack analytic skills. Each of the building blocks you identify at this point should be so unarguably important that a student's status regarding every building block must be *and will be* verified via formal or informal assessment. You are not trying to locate "nice to know" building blocks here. Rather, you are isolating "need to know" building blocks.

As noted earlier, a subskill is a lesser cognitive skill that students will need to have achieved before they can master the target curricular aim itself. For example, suppose you were trying to generate a learning progression underlying students' mastery of a high-level cognitive skill focused on the evaluation of the editorials found on the opinion pages of most daily newspapers. Well, one important subskill for this curriculum aim is for students to be able to distinguish between statements of fact and statements of opinion. Students who can't distinguish between factual statements and opinion statements will not be able to properly evaluate newspaper editorials.

Remember, the purpose of identifying subskills is so that you can identify students' mastery of them. You don't want to identify endless lists of subskills, and you do want to be sure that each is truly requisite. For example, the ability to judge the attention-arresting caliber of the editorial's headline might be a valuable subskill for students to acquire, but it's not genuinely essential to students' editorial-analysis skills. And if two or three of the subskills you are considering can be coalesced in the form of a single, larger-grain subskill, that's just fine. To illustrate, if you are teaching math students three different ways to correctly estimate the answers to word problems and it suits you to roll Estimation Technique *A*, Estimation Technique *B*, and Estimation Technique *C* into the single subskill of Common Estimation Techniques, go right ahead and do so.

The second kind of building block is a body of enabling knowledge. Such building blocks identify information that students must have in their possession if they are going to be successful in mastering the target curricular aim. As an example, think about how essay composition is built on an understanding of punctuation rules and the conventions of word usage. Each of these constitutes a separate body of enabling knowledge students must know, that is, must have memorized well enough to reproduce mentally or on a test. As was true with subskill building blocks, all building blocks that are bodies of enabling knowledge must be truly *necessary* for the student's mastery of the target curricular aim. And "nice to know" bodies of enabling knowledge no more have a place in a well-conceived learning progression than "nice to know" subskills do.

The way you get a fix on these building blocks is to focus clearly on the cognitive skill embodied in the target curricular aim and then work backward. Put to yourself a question such as the following: "In order for a student to really master the target curricular aim being sought in this instance, what subskills or enabling knowledge are absolutely necessary for that student to possess?" What you'll often discover is that once you have isolated a necessary subskill, you will discover the subskill itself has necessary precursors in the form of even lesser subskills or bodies of enabling knowledge that, in this instance, enable a student to accomplish a subskill en route to the student's ultimate mastery of the target curricular aim. Carried to its logical conclusion, once you being to engage in a backward analysis, you might end up all the way back to a student's ability to read, write, or tell the difference between two different letters of the alphabet. But what you are supposed to focus on when coming up with a learning progression is the set of building blocks linked directly to the target curricular aim for which you are generating that learning progression. In other words, the building blocks you will be identifying are the subskills and knowledge you will be addressing instructionally.

The natural tendency of most educators when they first begin to create learning progressions is to identify too many precursors and lay out far too many building blocks. It is better to end up with a small set of truly requisite precursory building blocks than to create a mind-numbing multitude of such building blocks.

What's my tip for determining if each of your potential building blocks is truly a requisite precursor? Ask yourself whether, if your students did not master it, you'd feel obliged to go back and teach them differently. In other words, is a building block so very important that you'd want to make an *adjustment decision* based on students' mastery or nonmastery of that particular building block? If you would regard the building block as so significant that, if unmastered, you'd really need to reteach it, then odds are that this particular building block is *really* requisite.

Step 2 typically requires the very hardest thinking in the entire four-step process, but once you've completed it, you're ready to screen your identified set of subskills and bodies of enabling knowledge against their "assessability potential." This is what's involved in Step 3, so let's look at it now.

Step 3. Determine whether it's possible to measure students' status with respect to each preliminarily identified building block. Sometimes it's easy to initially isolate a flock of subskills and bodies of enabling knowledge, but then you come to realize upon closer scrutiny that students' mastery of several of those building blocks will be difficult or downright impossible to assess. Accordingly, you need to go through each building block, one by one, and make sure there's a practical way of assessing students to determine their status regarding each building block you've identified. (In subsequent chapters, we will consider a wide range of potential assessment ploys, both formal and informal, for determining students' building-block mastery.)

There are several dividends associated with this third step in the building of learning progressions. For one thing, you may discover that it might be far too much trouble to actually measure students' status with respect to a given building block. Remember, the reason we are digging into learning progressions with such zeal is that they can provide a framework for the sorts of formative assessment activities that will take place in a classroom. Well, if one or more building blocks in a learning progression are essentially unmeasurable, you'll have created an assessment framework that is, at least in part, useless.

Another reason for considering the practicality of assessing students regarding each building block is that this intellectual exercise will typically help you acquire a fuller understanding of each building block involved. It's especially tempting to arrive at a fairly clear idea about what's entailed in a subskill or body of enabling knowledge, but "fairly clear" doesn't cut it when you're trying to generate a powerful learning progression. By carefully considering the assessment approach you could use with each building block, you'll not only reach a better understanding of those building blocks but may also discover that, barring Herculean effort, it will be impossible to assess students' status with respect to some of them.

As a consequence of Step 3, you should be confident that all of the subskills and bodies of enabling knowledge you've identified in Step 2 are, in fact, assessable. At that point, then, you're ready for the wrap-up action called for in Step 4.

Step 4. Arrange all building blocks in an instructionally defensible sequence. This final step in our approach calls for both analytic rigor and at least a dollop of pedagogical artistry. You'll need to place the progression's building blocks in the most sensible order from an instructional perspective. Sometimes that order will be obvious, especially when there's a specific chunk of knowledge students need to master in order to tackle a subskill explicitly based on such knowledge. Students couldn't, for example, make change from a one-dollar bill without first knowing the monetary value of pennies, nickels, dimes, quarters, and 50-cent pieces. In other cases, it may make no difference whether students learn Subskill X before Subskill Y. Does it really matter whether a student learns how to determine the median of a set of test scores before learning how to determine the mean of those scores? And in some instances, there will be a judgmentally discernible "best order" for students to try to master a learning progression's building blocks, hinging on your own pedagogical preferences and your ideas about how children in general and your students in particular are most likely to learn the particular content being taught.

As you sequence the building blocks in your learning progression, remember that you'll need to set aside classroom time to assess students' status with respect to each building block. These built-in time allowances might influence the order you ultimately choose, because the need to carry out complete building-block assessments could prevent you from spending instructional time on interesting or engaging topics of borderline significance. For example, what seemed like a sensible sequence of building blocks when there was time for the introduction of several borderline topics that would have helped students as they transitioned from one building block to another might need to be resequenced when those borderline topics must be omitted. But when Step 4 is reduced to its essentials, it really means you need to ask yourself what is the best order in which most students should learn the set of subskills and knowledge set forth in the building blocks you've identified. And, when you've done that, you're finished!

Be sure to remember that any learning progression you develop, however well thought out and carefully constructed, is incapable of being anything but your best-guess hypothesis of the sequenced precursors that lead, step by step, to students' mastery of an important curricular aim. First-version learning progressions frequently need some serious reworking, and you will need to keep a close watch on any learning progression you develop to see, over time, whether it seems to be appropriate. You may discover there are certain building blocks that are unnecessary or that there are some missing building blocks that need to be inserted. Don't be afraid to jiggle a learning progression so it seems likely to work better. Any shame you might feel about initially "getting it wrong" will be eclipsed by pride when the new and improved version leads your students to mastery.

Even though learning progressions should play a prominent role in the formative assessment process, if you set out to locate information regarding such progressions, you'll find few resources. A noteworthy exception is the highly readable analysis of learning progressions by Heritage (2007). This practitioner-oriented report provides both practical guidelines for building learning progressions and a number of illustrative progressions.

Mrs. Ballard Builds a Learning Progression

I want to conclude this look at learning progressions with a brief description of the learning progression a high school English teacher, Mrs. Ballard, creates for key cognitive skills she wants her students to master. Although this account is completely fictitious, I've built the description around the efforts of Mrs. Ballard because my most effective English teacher when I was a high-schooler was, you guessed it, Mrs. Ballard. As you will see, our fictitious Mrs. Ballard employs all steps in the previously described four-step strategy for building a learning progression. And because she's modeled after *my* Mrs. Ballard, she does so with a smile on her fictional face.

The Setting

Mrs. Ballard teaches English to juniors and seniors in an urban high school and also serves as her school's debate coach. As a consequence, the school's principal has allowed Mrs. Ballard to encourage prospective debaters to enroll in her English classes where, in addition to the state-specified curricular outcomes topics, they will learn more about the fundamentals of formal, competitive debate. Mrs. Ballard's students perform consistently well when the school's debate team competes at the annual county and state championships. Two years ago, one of her debate teams placed second in the entire state.

The Target Curricular Aim: Proactive Rebuttal Mitigation

The format of high school debate features a constructive presentation by members of one team followed by the opposing team's rebuttal presentation, typically focused on negating the previously presented position. It's appropriate, then, that one of Mrs. Ballard's debate-related curricular aims is the following: "Debaters will, prior to their opponents' rebuttal presentations, be able to proactively weaken the chief points in those forthcoming rebuttals."

Mrs. Ballard actually regards this debate-related cognitive skill as an important life skill. As she tells her students, in any sort of significant disagreement between individuals, those who can identify an opponent's likely points of attack and then eviscerate or weaken those points in advance will prevail more often than will those who allow rebuttal points to be leveled without advance repudiation.

Before sitting down to design a learning progression for this curricular aim, Mrs. Ballard devotes some up-front thinking time to the two preliminary considerations related to the number of building blocks and the grain size of those blocks. When it comes to learning progressions, her personal preference leans toward the lean. She would rather focus on a small number of large-grain building blocks that require a meaningful hunk of instructional time than take on a large number of small-grain building blocks she might teach more quickly.

The first step in the general learning-progression construction process is for the teacher to acquire a thorough understanding of the target curricular aim. This is the point at which a teacher who didn't have Mrs. Ballard's years of experience as a debate coach might find it useful to imagine behavior-difference situations in which students who possessed the skill of proactive rebuttal mitigation would respond differently from those students who didn't possess that skill. Mrs. Ballard, who is well versed in the nuances of competitive high school debating, has thought a lot about the key requirements underlying proactive rebuttal mitigation. She knows how she'll go about measuring student's mastery of this important skill: by observing the frequency with which her students employ it during their initial presentations in all of their practice and competition debates. She also plans to appraise the effectiveness of students' proactive repudiations. In other words, Mrs. Ballard decides to use what are, essentially, ongoing performance tests to determine whether students have mastered this target curricular aim.

Three Preliminary Subskills

The second step in constructing a learning progression is to identify all requisite precursory subskills and bodies of enabling knowledge. Mrs. Ballard knows that debaters must be cognizant of the content of any topics considered eligible for debate, and she knows that almost all of her students will immerse themselves in such content. Class discussions will alert her as to which students are sufficiently knowledgeable and which students aren't sufficiently knowledgeable about each debate topic's key content. Having considered the matter of related content mastery, she proceeds to focus on the skills students absolutely must have in order to master proactive rebuttal mitigation. Mrs. Ballard uses a process of backward analysis wherein she starts off with the skill being sought of students, then mentally analyzes what sorts of precursor skills and knowledge students need in order to acquire that skill. Ultimately, she generates the following list:

- *Subskill 1: Analysis.* Students must be able to analyze their own positions and identify the most significant points of vulnerability in those positions.
- *Subskill 2: Damage Control.* Students can create effective ways of minimizing the damage that would ensue if opponents' rebuttals address these points of vulnerability.

• *Subskill 3: Subtle Infusion.* Students can structure their initial debate presentations to subtly incorporate in-advance weakening of their opponents' attacks.

Assessing Subskill Mastery

With her preliminary set of building blocks established, Mrs. Ballard goes to on Step 3 in the construction process: determining whether it's possible to measure students' status with respect to each building block. Remember, students' mastery or nonmastery of a learning progression's building blocks at the heart of the formative assessment process; if Mrs. Ballard can't assess students' status with respect to the three building blocks, the process won't work.

Because debaters must be prepared to defend either side of a proposition, Mrs. Ballard wants to see how well her students can display these three subskills irrespective of which side of an argument they are asked to defend. Her plan is to select information describing the pro and con sides of a debate topic used in a previous year, ask students to become conversant with the content and, having done so, provide a three-section written analysis for both sides of the proposition. In each of those analyses they are to (1) identify potential weaknesses, (2) create damage-minimization tactics, and (3) describe ways of effectively infusing these tactics into a debater's opening presentation. With this three-part test, she can assess students' mastery of all three subskills at one time. She could also split apart the three subskills so that each one is assessed separately in brief constructed-response quizzes. Mrs. Ballard has used these sorts of constructed-response, short-answer assessments in the past (always using previously unencountered debate topics), and she believes the assessment approach works quite satisfactorily.

Sequencing the Building Blocks

The final step in constructing a learning progression is to arrange all building blocks in an instructionally defensible sequence.

Mrs. Ballard reviews her building blocks and decides that her original numerical sequence of the three subskills is eminently logical: Students need to first spot weaknesses in their own cases, next figure out how to deflect attacks aimed at those weaknesses, and, finally, devise ways of adroitly incorporating such damage-control information into their initial presentations.

With her learning progression now set, Mrs. Ballard begins her instruction, feeling confident that this approach will provide her students with the skills they need to become expert proactive rebuttal mediators and provide her with assessment evidence she needs to ensure students' mastery.

So, that's a run-through of how I am sure my treasured Mrs. Ballard would have played the learning-progression game had there been, way back then, a learning-progression game to play. And in the course of instruction, if she had discovered that there were deficits in the learning progression she had devised, then she'd surely have rethought and revised that progression. Remember, learning progressions are really hypotheses that may or may not work out as planned. However, because this is my fictitious vignette, and Mrs. Ballard was my nonfictional favorite teacher, I'm positive hers would have been flawless!

SUPER-SUCCINCT SUMMARY

- A learning progression is a sequenced set of subskills and bodies of knowledge it is believed students must master en route to mastering a more remote curricular aim.

- Learning progressions provide guidance to teachers regarding what to assess and when to assess it as part of the formative assessment process.

- Elaborate learning progressions may be instructionally helpful for some teachers, but teachers must be sure to assess students' mastery of all building blocks in a learning progression.

- When constructing learning progressions, teachers should select a building-block grain size that best meshes with their tolerance for detail.

- A four-step strategy for building learning progressions consists of (1) thoroughly understanding the target curricular aim, (2) identifying all requisite precursory subskills and bodies of enabling knowledge, (3) determining whether students' status with respect to each preliminarily identified building block can be measured, and (4) arranging all building blocks in an instructionally defensible sequence.

Level 1 Formative Assessment

Teachers' Instructional Adjustments

[Chapter Preview]

• The four levels of formative assessment

• The distinction between instructional activities and formative assessment activities

• The four steps of Level 1 formative assessment, a strategy for improving the caliber of instruction

THERE'S MORE THAN ONE WAY TO CARVE A TURKEY OR TO CUT up a cake; both conventional wisdom and turkey-carving and cake-cutting experience tell us so. Similarly, there's more than one way to chop up the world of formative assessment.

This chapter and the three following it focus on four distinctive applications of formative assessment. Although these four "levels" were fleetingly identified in the book's preface, before we launch into this chapter's close examination of Level 1 formative assessment, it will be useful to pause and consider Figure 3.1's overview of the distinguishing features of all four levels.

Figure 3.1	The Four Levels of Formative Assessment

Level 1: Teachers' Instructional Adjustments

Teachers collect evidence by which they decide whether to adjust their current or immediately-upcoming instruction in order to improve the effectiveness of that instruction.

Level 2: Students' Learning Tactic Adjustments

Students use evidence of their current skills-and-knowledge status to decide whether to adjust the procedures they're using in an effort to learn something.

Level 3: Classroom Climate Shift

Teachers consistently apply formative assessment to the degree that its use transforms a traditional, comparison-dominated classroom, where the main purpose of assessment is to assign grades, into an atypical, learning-dominated classroom, where the main purpose of assessment is to improve the quality of teaching and learning.

Level 4: Schoolwide Implementation

An entire school (or district) adopts one or more levels of formative assessment, chiefly through the use of professional development and teacher learning communities.

About now, you might be saying to yourself that yes, turkeys must be carved (unless one is ravenous) and cakes must be cut (unless one is gluttonous), but why is there any need to subdivide formative assessment into different levels? My response is that dividing formative assessment into functions fundamentally distinguishable from one another is a useful way to bring additional clarity to this important topic. It reinforces educators' understanding of how formative assessment can bear on the day-to-day activities of teachers, students, and school administrators.

It's almost time to begin examining Level 1 formative assessment in detail, but before we do that, it will be helpful to focus a bit more on the difference between classroom formative assessment and classroom instruction.

Instruction and Formative Assessment: Not the Same

In Chapter 1, we settled on a definition of formative assessment and looked at how formative assessment, if used properly, can become a powerful contributor to a teacher's instructional decision making. But formative assessment is *not* the same thing as instruction.

Instruction refers to the set of teacher-determined activities carried out in an effort to get students to accomplish a curricular outcome. Using this definition, instruction is the *means* by which a teacher's students attain a curricular *end.* Therefore, formative assessment can be regarded accurately as a process intended to make a teacher's instructional means more effective. Yes, instruction can be genuinely effective even if there is no formative assessment involved. I would argue, though, and I have, that formative assessment will usually help make instruction better because it's about using evidence of students' mastery status to make instructional adjustments *if* the evidence suggests those adjustments are warranted.

To illustrate, let's assume a particularly competent teacher has designed a one-month instructional unit to promote students' mastery of a really high-level cognitive skill. The teacher (we'll call her Jill) plans to undertake the following activities during the unit:

1. Fully clarify for students the nature of the cognitive skill they're supposed to master by the time they achieve the unit's target curricular aim.

2. Motivate students to master the target curricular aim by showing them how their acquisition of the cognitive skill will be *personally* beneficial.

3. Supply instruction regarding any key building blocks students must possess en route to their acquisition of the unit's targeted skill.

4. Model the use of the skill while explaining to students how she does so.

5. Give students ample guided practice as well as independent practice in their use of the targeted cognitive skill.

What I've just described is a reasonably well-conceived instructional design. If Jill implements this instructional design the way she plans to, odds are that it's going to work; after a month's worth of instruction, all (or almost all) of Jill's students will probably have mastered the high-level cognitive skill being sought. Jill's instructional design will be successful even though there might not be even one whiff of formative assessment involved.

So instruction, if properly conceptualized and skillfully implemented, can be effective without any formative assessment whatsoever. *But it is less likely to be,* and here's why. The function of formative assessment is to help teachers and students decide whether they need to make any adjustments in what they're doing. If a teacher's instruction is dazzlingly wonderful, and if students' learning tactics are marvelously appropriate, then no adjustments are needed. But dazzlingly wonderful instruction and marvelously appropriate learning tactics are usually the exception rather than the rule. Many teachers' instructional procedures and many students' learning tactics need major or minor adjustments. Because formative assessment can help teachers and students decide whether adjustments *should* be made, it can send one of two helpful messages to teachers and students. Message 1 is, "No adjustments are needed!" Message 2 is, "Adjustments are most definitely needed!" In short, formative assessment serves as a sensible monitoring strategy for both teachers and students.

Should teachers attempt to design wondrously fine instructional activities for their students? Of course they should. Should students set out to employ the most effective tactics they can use when trying to learn things? Of course they should. But because formative assessment will supply assessment-based evidence indicating whether teachers and students "got it right," it can play an important role in helping teachers and students monitor the effectiveness of their efforts.

Even though classroom instruction and formative assessment are different, both of these activities are focused on the same outcome: improved student learning. From a teacher's perspective, it makes sense to design the very best instruction possible but, thereafter, monitor the quality of those planned instructional activities to see if they ought to be altered. Formative assessment activities should be sitting smack in the middle of a teacher's instructional-monitoring strategy. And this constitutes the first of our four levels of formative assessment, namely, the level focused on *teachers' instructional adjustments*.

One Mission, Four Activities

Level 1 formative assessment's goal is simple: to help teachers decide whether they need to adjust what they're currently doing instructionally or what they plan to do next instructionally. Those adjustments might take place immediately—by tweaking a lesson that's currently under way, for example; or they might deal with an upcoming lesson: the next day's lesson or several lessons planned for the near future. Let's turn now to four steps, displayed in Figure 3.2, that teachers must take to engage effectively in Level 1 formative assessment.

Step 1: Identify Adjustment Occasions

Teachers often make on-the-spot instructional adjustments. If, in the middle of Mr. Howell's explanation to his class of 4th graders, he takes students' glazed-over expressions as a hint that this particular segment of his explanation is confusing, he is likely to make an instant decision to return to that apparently murky explanation in order to do a better explanatory job. Such on-the-spot adjustments are usually defensible because teachers have a

Figure 3.2 | Teachers' Level 1 Steps

Step 1: Identify adjustment occasions.
The teacher decides when, during an instructional sequence, adjustment decisions should be made.

Step 2: Select assessments.
The teacher chooses the formal or informal assessment procedures to be used for each adjustment occasion.

Step 3: Establish adjustment triggers.
The teacher determines, in advance, what level of student performance will necessitate an instructional adjustment.

Step 4: Make instructional adjustments.
The teacher makes any necessary adjustments.

way of inferring that such instant changes will be beneficial. These sorts of adjustments, though commendable, are not what the first step of Level 1 formative assessment is all about. Instead, adjustment occasions to be identified in this first step are *the most significant choice-points associated with students' movement toward mastery of the target curricular aim.*

To identify the specific occasions when a teacher should decide whether to adjust instruction, the teacher should look to the learning progression developed for the curricular aim being pursued. Remember, learning progressions are specifically intended to isolate the requisite building blocks (subskills and bodies of enabling knowledge) that students will need to master on their way to full-fledged mastery of the target curricular aim. Accordingly, it makes sense for teachers to try to get a fix on their students' status with respect to each of those building blocks. But when?

This is where a teacher needs to exercise some pedagogical savvy by deciding at what point, in relation to a specific building block, to collect assessment data. Figure 3.3 represents the situation graphically.

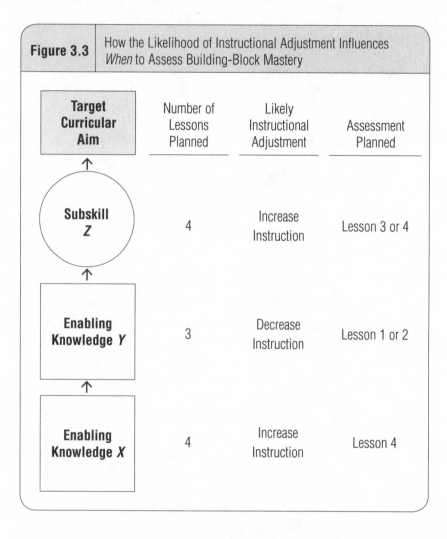

Figure 3.3	How the Likelihood of Instructional Adjustment Influences *When* to Assess Building-Block Mastery		
Target Curricular Aim	Number of Lessons Planned	Likely Instructional Adjustment	Assessment Planned
Subskill Z	4	Increase Instruction	Lesson 3 or 4
Enabling Knowledge Y	3	Decrease Instruction	Lesson 1 or 2
Enabling Knowledge X	4	Increase Instruction	Lesson 4

In the figure you see a learning progression containing only three building blocks, two of which are bodies of enabling knowledge and one of which is a subskill. The number of lessons the teacher plans to devote to each of the three building blocks is listed in the column to the immediate right. In the next column are the teacher's judgments about the probable nature of the learning progression adjustment that will be made for each building block: whether it is likely that students will need more instruction (owing to low levels of mastery) or less instruction (owing to high levels of mastery). As you can see, for two building blocks (Enabling Knowledge X and Subskill Z), the teacher estimates that if there are adjustments to be made, those adjustments will call for *additional* instruction. In the remaining building block (Enabling Knowledge Y), the teacher judges that less instruction, that is, fewer lessons, may be required in order for students to acquire the needed enabling knowledge. In a sense, the teacher is predicting whether students will find individual building blocks more or less challenging to master. The "difficulty level" of particular building blocks reflects the teacher's judgment about a building block's complexity and breadth. Finally, in the right-hand column of the figure you can see the teacher's decision about when to assess students' status with respect to each of the three building blocks.

Figure 3.3 illustrates how the two most common adjustment options should play a prominent role in a teacher's decision about *when* to assess students within the instructional segment devoted to mastery of a given building block. Most frequently, an adjustment requires *more instruction* (often different from the instruction previously used) because the evidence collected from students indicates that too many of them haven't yet mastered the particular building block involved. If the teacher believes that students are likely to need additional instruction on a particular building block, it makes sense to collect pertinent assessment evidence in the latter phases or near the very end of instruction. In this way, if more instruction is needed, the teacher can supply it immediately without having already moved ahead to a subsequent building block. Notice, for instance, that because the Figure 3.3 teacher thinks the likely instructional adjustment for Subskill Z and Enabling Knowledge X will call for increased instruction, the plan is to collect formative assessment evidence at or near the close of the allotted instructional time.

The other most common instructional adjustment teachers make when focusing on building-block mastery is *less instruction*, that is, to decrease the amount of instruction focused on a particular building block. In Figure 3.3, you see that the teacher thinks students are likely to need less instruction focused on Enabling Knowledge *Y* and plans accordingly to collect formative assessment evidence early in the treatment of this specific building block: during the first or second lesson of the three lessons planned. If students' assessment evidence indicates they've acquired Enabling Knowledge *Y* by that point, the teacher can immediately move on to the next building block in the progression.

To review, teachers need to examine the building blocks in a learning progression, judge the most probable adjustment they will need to make (more instruction or less instruction), and then time their formative assessments appropriately: *assessing late* in a building block's treatment whether *more instruction* seems likely or *assessing early* in a building block's treatment if *less instruction* seems likely. Incidentally, this guideline applies to single-lesson treatments of a building block as well as multi-lesson treatments. Will teachers always make the right judgments regarding the likely nature of all necessary instructional adjustments? Of course they won't. But if teachers exercise their best pedagogical judgment regarding the nature of a likely adjustment, then they'll do a better job timing the collection of assessment data than they would if they *hadn't* given the matter any thought.

There's one final decision a teacher must make about adjustment occasions: whether to go ahead and assess students' attainment of the target curricular aim itself during the latter stages of the instruction aimed at that curricular aim. The timing of this kind of "final rehearsal" exam is set so that there's sufficient time to double back and address any shortcomings students seem to have with regard to their mastery of the target curricular aim. Most educators' decision about whether to do this or not depends on the stakes associated with their students' performances. Two situations in which a rehearsal exam is most often thought to be appropriate are when the public perception of a school's success rests on students' scores on an annual accountability test and when a student's diploma is riding on the score achieved on a high school exit exam.

Remember, the function of Level 1 formative assessment is to allow the teacher to arrive at valid inferences regarding students' building block mastery status so that the teacher, now able to determine if students have satisfactorily mastered a given building block, can decide whether to alter any current instructional plans. Remember also that the assessment procedures to be employed in Level 1 formative assessment need not be formal "tests." (We'll deal with this in just a minute.) No, the first step of Level 1 formative assessment requires teachers to look forward into their instructional plans—whether those plans cover only a single lesson, a multiweek instructional unit, or an entire academic year—and identify those occasions when assessment-based evidence will be collected in order to decide whether to alter planned instruction.

The teacher's decisions should be guided by a previously constructed learning progression, and care must be taken at this point not to aim at too many adjustment occasions. Back in Chapter 1, I noted that the main impediment to properly functioning formative assessment is teachers' reluctance to use it. A teacher who identifies what seems to be a burdensome number of adjustment occasions is unlikely to employ formative assessment for very long.

Step 2: Select Assessments

The second step for teachers implementing Level 1 formative assessment pertains to the choice of assessment procedures they will employ. This is a difficult step to carry out, not only because there are so many assessment options available but also because a teacher who chooses the "wrong" assessment procedures is probably going to draw invalid inferences about students' mastery status. Invalid inferences almost always lead to unsound instructional decisions. Another path to invalid inferences is incomplete sampling: asking too few questions or asking those questions of too few students. The more significant the adjustment decision, the more assessment evidence teachers should consider and the greater the proportion of students who will need to supply this evidence. Let's look now at some of the assessment options.

Traditional assessment procedures. When it comes to determining how well students have mastered a particular subskill or a body of enabling knowledge, teachers have all the traditional assessment tools at their disposal. They might employ *selected-response items,* such as multiple-choice or true/false items, and also *constructed-response items,* such as short-answer items or essay items.

Because testing time takes away from teaching time, there is an instructional advantage to using shorter rather than longer tests. Nonetheless, any assessment used during this phase of formative assessment must contain enough items so that the sampling of students' knowledge and skills it measures is sufficient to help the teacher make valid inferences about what individual students know and can do. If there are too few items, odds are greater that the teacher will draw an invalid inference from the performance data, concluding erroneously that students have or have not mastered the building block to an acceptable degree.

Teachers who need some assistance with traditional testing techniques have many first-rate resources available to them. Essentially every classroom assessment textbook widely available today describes a full array of conventional assessment techniques, and most also contain a number of experience-based guidelines about how to construct suitable selected-response and constructed-response items. With those traditional assessment approaches well covered elsewhere, I'd like to focus here on several less traditional assessment ploys that teachers have found useful in the collection of formative assessment evidence.

Letter-card responses. This procedure is a quick-turnaround variation of the tried-and-true selected-response assessment. It calls for giving every student a set of white index cards. Each set contains seven cards, and each card is clearly and boldly marked with one of the following letters: *A, B, C, D, E, T,* and *F.* (If you're in the mood, you can also toss in an eighth card, marked with a question mark.) Instead of sampling students' building block mastery with a written, 10-item multiple-choice or true/false quiz, the teacher reads one or two of these items out loud (or presents them on a chalkboard or via a projection system) and asks students to respond by holding up a card with their response at an appropriate signal, such as "on the count of three." The teacher's quick scrutiny of students' responses will indicate whether most students seem to be "getting it" and, if not, where they seem to be having misunderstandings. If one-third of the class is holding up the *C* card when the correct multiple-choice response is *A,* it's clear that content related to both the *A* response and the *C* response needs additional instructional attention. The *T* and the *F* cards allow this letter-card procedure to work for true/false items, and the optional question mark provides students a way to accurately convey their uncertainty instead of going for the "lucky guess" or, in the case of true/false items, making a lucky guess about half the time.

Use of letter-cards is one of several *all-student response procedures* in which every student is obligated to supply an answer to every question posed during a lesson. Even if there were no formative assessment involved, the virtue of all-student response schemes is that they tend to keep students mentally plugged into what's going on in class.

Key questioning during discussion. Another similar but different all-student response procedure teachers can use to foster engagement in a lesson's activities is *random-response Q&A.* This technique calls for the teacher to present a question to the class and select a student at random to answer the question. A good way to do this is to write each student's name on a tongue depressor or popsicle stick and select one from the collection after posing the question. If the "chosen" student's response is unsatisfactory, the teacher chooses another student's "name-stick." As a consequence, all students must be prepared to answer every question. Many other variations on this procedure are possible, but what's important is that every student has an equal opportunity to be selected as the designated question answerer on all occasions.

Although the random-response Q&A procedure represents an excellent way of keeping students tuned in to what's transpiring in class, it would *not* be an appropriate procedure for a teacher to use when collecting evidence for an adjustment decision. To arrive at a defensible adjustment decision, a teacher needs to make an inference about how *most* students in the class are doing with respect to each building block in a learning progression; the status of just one or two students isn't insignificant, but within the formative assessment process it isn't sufficient to support instructional adjustment decisions. Thus, for example, during a teacher-led class discussion, much of the discussion session could be peppered with random-response Q&A procedures, but when the teacher needs to collect adjustment-influencing evidence, such evidence should be gathered using all-student response procedures, such as letter-cards.

A properly engineered class discussion for purposes of formative assessment will usually revolve around a handful of key questions intended to supply the crucial evidence a teacher needs to arrive at an adjustment decision. These pivotal adjustment-influencing questions must be carefully conceptualized *before* the class session in which the discussion will take place. Remember, formative assessment is a *planned* process. Teachers can't expect to come up with excellent adjustment-influencing questions on the spur of the moment.

Whiteboard responses. The letter-card response approach is a good one, but it does limit the teacher to selected-response items wherein students need only choose an answer from a list of options. This drawback can be easily addressed by supplying each student with an erasable whiteboard, roughly 8 by 12 inches in size. (These are available at a nominal cost from school supply stores or office supply stores.) Using the same general approach as that described for use with letter-card responses, students are presented with short-answer items for which a single word or a brief phrase would be an appropriate response. After having written their responses in large, visible-to-the-teacher words, students hold up their whiteboards when told to do so. The teacher scans the responses and makes an evidence-based inference about the students' mastery levels. At the teacher's prompt, students must erase their boards to be ready for the next question. Many teachers who are adept at using whiteboards in their classes ask students to bring in a clean sock to use as an eraser.

Success with this method requires the teacher to become adept at framing questions to which short-answer responses are suitable. If the responses sought are too lengthy to fit on the whiteboards or to be scanned and processed quickly, then a more traditional paper-and-pencil test is probably a better choice.

The traffic-signal technique. The essence of the approaches described so far is to provide the teacher with assessment-elicited evidence regarding students' mastery of the key building blocks underlying a target curricular aim (or, possibly, mastery of the curricular aim itself). But there's another way of helping a teacher arrive at a judgment regarding the same issue, and it depends on students' *self-declared level of understanding.* Here's how this technique works.

First, the teacher supplies each student with a set of three paper or plastic cups. One of the cups is green, one is yellow, and one is red. Students stack the cups upside down on their desks (or workspaces) with the red cup at the bottom, the yellow cup on top of the red, and the green cup on top of the yellow. At the beginning of the activity, all students' "top cups" are green.

During segments of instruction specifically designated for the traffic-signal technique, students use their stacked cups to represent their personal level of understanding regarding what's being treated in class. If a student leaves the green cup on top, it signifies, "I understand this, and I understand it well enough so that I could explain it to other students if I'm asked to do so." If a yellow cup is on top, the student sends the message, "I'm somewhat unsure about whether I understand what's going on now." A red cup on top indicates, "I really don't understand what's being treated at the moment."

Students need to get used to employing this sort of traffic-signal technique, of course, and it usually takes several days for them to become comfortable with it. Many teachers find it is beneficial to occasionally ask a "green-cupper" to explain a concept to the rest of the class. Without such an occasional request for a green-cupper's explanation, students might be inclined to simply hide behind the alleged understanding their green cups signify. When a teacher begins to see a preponderance of yellow or red cups in class, the teacher's inference should be quite clear: Students are having trouble understanding what's going on. This signals the need for an adjustment in the way that the teacher is explaining or modeling the topic at hand.

When we turn, in Chapter 4, to Level 2 formative assessment, which focuses on students' decisions regarding their own learning tactics, the traffic-signal technique can play a particularly important and constructive role for students' decision making. When used during Level 1 formative assessment, it supplies teachers with nearly instantaneous insights regarding their students' self-signified levels of understanding.

Item sampling. Decisions about whether to make an instructional adjustment don't always require teachers to assess every student in class. What the teacher is often looking for is a reasonably accurate *estimate* of the status of the entire class with respect to students' mastery of what's being assessed. Because this is the case, teachers may find *item sampling* to be both an efficient and sensible formative assessment procedure.

Item sampling consists of a teacher administering only a portion of a test's items to a portion of the students in class. By amalgamating the sampled results, the teacher can obtain a defensible estimate of the entire class's level of mastery in far less time than it would have taken had all students been obliged to complete all of a test's items.

For example, suppose you are a geometry teacher trying to get a fix on your students' abilities to compute the areas of diverse sorts of geometric shapes. Let's say you have created 20 test items covering the range of geometric shapes for which students might compute areas. However, rather than creating a single 20-item test, you randomly put the 20 items into 5 separate, 4-item "testlets." You then randomly administer the 5 testlets to different students in your 30-student class so that 6 students will complete each 4-item testlet. To get a reasonably accurate estimate of the entire class's performance on the full 20-item test, you simply aggregate all of the students' performances on the testlets. The resulting performance estimate, the average for the entire class, is usually accurate enough for the kinds of adjustment decisions required in most formative assessment settings. It's an especially useful procedure for teachers who are reluctant to devote gobs of class time to assessment.

To review, Step 2 of Level 1 formative assessment is for the teacher to decide what assessment procedures will be employed to collect the evidence bearing on potential instructional adjustments. It's here that the teacher transforms preliminary thinking about how to assess students' mastery of the building blocks and the target curricular aim as a whole, done during the learning progression's conceptualization, into actual assessment decisions.

Step 3: Establish Adjustment Triggers

The third step teachers should follow when implementing Level 1 formative assessment arises from the teacher's need to decide whether, based on the assessment-elicited evidence, instructional adjustments should be made. It's one thing to collect evidence regarding students' building-block status. It's quite another thing to arrive at an "adjust" or "don't adjust" decision. To help a teacher make this significant decision, Step 3 calls for the teacher, *in advance of the actual assessment*, to arrive at a decision regarding the levels of students' performance that would lead the teacher to make an instructional adjustment.

An example of the sort of *adjustment trigger* that might be set at this point in the formative assessment process would be when a geography teacher decides, "If at least 75 percent of my students do *not* earn scores of 80 percent or better on tomorrow's map-usage exam, I'll adjust the next lesson so we intensively review basic map-usage procedures." As you can see from this example, the teacher sets an adjustment-trigger level by identifying (1) a required level of individual-student performance as well as (2) a required level of total-group performance. Individually, a student needs to earn a score of 80 percent or better on the map-usage test. However, if at least 75 percent of the students do not attain that 80-percent correct score, then there will be an instructional adjustment.

As shown in Figure 3.4, a predetermined adjustment trigger requires a teacher to establish, *before* collecting assessment evidence from students, (1) a minimum per-student performance level and (2) a minimum per-class performance level, that is, the percentage of students who must achieve the minimum per-student performance level.

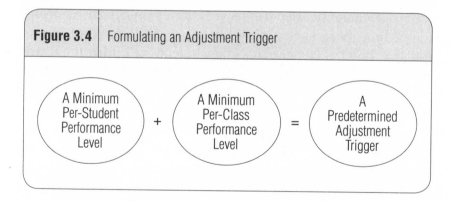

Figure 3.4 | Formulating an Adjustment Trigger

Although a teacher needs to set both per-student and per-class levels in order to establish an adjustment trigger, the nature of the likely adjustment to be made will influence the nature of the adjustment-trigger statement. Remember, almost all instructional adjustments boil down to "more instruction" or "less instruction" regarding the building blocks for mastering the target curricular aim. Thus, the trigger statement is likely to resemble one of the two examples that follow.

To *increase* instruction:
"If at least 90 percent of my students don't earn scores of 90 percent or better on Thursday's formative quiz, I'll add a new review lesson on Friday."

To *decrease* instruction:
"If at least 95 percent of my students correctly answer at least 8 of tomorrow's 10-item quiz on Topic *X*, I will delete next week's planned Topic *X* review lesson."

TO ADJUST, OR NOT TO ADJUST?

If Shakespeare had turned his mind to it, he probably could have supplied great advice about how a teacher should decide whether an instructional adjustment is warranted in the midst of an ongoing teaching sequence. But Hamlet stopped with "To be, or not to be," so for the question of "To adjust or not to adjust?" we need to come up with our own answer.

I was wrestling with this question at the same time that I was lucky enough to lead two one-day workshops in the Kyrene School District near Phoenix, Arizona. I'm indebted to my Kyrene colleagues for helping me sharpen some of my thinking related to formative assessment. They were particularly insightful when I asked them how they arrived at a yes-or-no decision about whether to adjust their own instructional activities.

I presented the following problem, then asked for their help in coming up with a defensible answer: "Imagine you are teaching a 4th grade class, using erasable whiteboards as a formative tool during a content presentation. At certain points of the lesson, you pause to pose a short-answer question related to the content just covered, and each student writes a response and holds it up for review. What percent of your students would need to answer a question incorrectly for you to decide you should adjust your instruction?"

After a bit of discussion among themselves, the Kyrene educators pointed out that a teacher couldn't set this adjustment trigger without first determining the importance of the content treated in the specific question. If the question dealt with something really important, then incorrect responses from as little as 10 percent of students might indicate the need for an instructional adjustment. With less important content, incorrect responses of up to 40 percent might not warrant an adjustment. The Kyrene educators said, in a nutshell, "The more important the content, the smaller the percent of erroneous students it should take to spur an instructional adjustment."

As a guideline, this makes a lot of sense—and no less an authority than Dylan Wiliam agrees. At a conference we both attended, I took the opportunity to ask him how many students a teacher must assess so as to come up with a solid decision about whether or not to adjust instruction. Without hesitation, and with a British accent that in and of itself commanded deference, Dylan replied, "Between 80 and 20 percent, depending on the gravity of the adjustment decision being faced." The more serious the adjustment decision at hand, the greater the proportion of students who need to be assessed.

I like this 80–20 rule of thumb a lot. Nonetheless, I am sure that in an instance when a teacher might have collected assessment evidence from an entire class, Dylan would not suggest discarding the 20-percent "overage." It's the Scots who have a reputation for being hyper-thrifty. Dylan is Welsh.

Establishment of minimum per-student and per-class performance levels is no easy task. It is challenging for teachers to come up with the performance levels that will oblige them to adjust or not adjust an instructional plan before they give an assessment. But if teachers make a good-faith effort to arrive at what they regard as reasonable per-student and per-class performance levels, those teachers will typically make better adjustment decisions than if they had simply collected formative assessment data, then tried to arrive at an after-the-fact adjustment decision once the assessment evidence had been collected. There's typically too much temptation for teachers to "go along" with the assessment data, making no adjustments at all because "that's just how the students performed."

Can a teacher, after having formally set a predetermined adjustment trigger, *change* that trigger? Of course. Formative assessment's function is to improve learning, and if assessment-based evidence suggests that a preset adjustment trigger is strikingly out of whack with reality, then those trigger levels must be modified.

Step 4: Make Instructional Adjustments

The final step in Level 1 formative assessment is for teachers to actually make adjustments in instruction. It is always possible, of course, for no adjustments to be needed, but that sort of scenario is not very common. Far more often than not, students' formative assessment evidence will let teachers know an instructional modification is necessary. Sometimes those adjustments will be minor, resembling a bit of tinkering and polishing more than a major overhaul. But there will also be instances when profound instructional adjustments are required. Whether major or minor, adjustments in a teacher's instructional design typically require the teacher to draw on personal pedagogical expertise. Here's where teachers need to show just how instructionally astute they really are. This is the moment when top teachers shine.

When the evidence suggests that a set of lessons is working even more effectively that foreseen, it's not too tough to figure out what to do. *Deleting* a planned instructional segment is the easiest adjustment to make. The challenging adjustments are those needed when the planned instruction hasn't worked as well as expected. Typically, a teacher's instructional plan reflects that teacher's best bet about how to get students to achieve the target curricular aim or an en route building block. So, when the assessment evidence, be it formal test data or informal assessment evidence such as traffic-signal data, indicates that *more* instruction is needed, what should that "more instruction" be?

One of the best places to start when considering potential add-ons to an instructional sequence is to revisit the original learning progression created for the curricular aim or building block under consideration. In reviewing that progression, were certain subskills or bodies of enabling knowledge overlooked, which, in hindsight, now seem crucial? When students are stumbling on a particular building block, are there aspects of this building block that haven't been treated instructionally or haven't been treated sufficiently? Are there any building blocks that, though interesting, are not really essential and, therefore, may be confusing students?

The next thing for a teacher to consider is whether the current instruction could have simply been done differently and, possibly, better. This is a moment when collegial consultation often pays off, big time. If a teacher asks another teacher for some ideas about how to tackle a particular topic or skill, the suggestions of a colleague can often be remarkably helpful.

Because the number of curricular aims a teacher might be pursuing is almost infinite, it's impossible to lay out here the best kinds of instructional adjustments to make when such adjustments are warranted. However, if students' assessment data indicate that current instruction isn't getting the job done, then almost any reasonable instructional adjustment has the potential to improve the situation, including changes in the way the teacher presents the material, represents its core ideas, articulates day-to-day objectives, groups students, and designs guided and independent practice activities. Clearly, the more pedagogical prowess a teacher can bring to the adjustment altar, the better.

SUPER-SUCCINCT SUMMARY

- Formative assessment can be divided into four cumulative applications: Level 1, in which teachers decide whether to adjust their current or immediately upcoming instruction in order to improve the effectiveness of that instruction; Level 2, in which students decide whether to adjust their learning tactics; Level 3, in which the teacher focuses on bringing about a classroom climate shift; and Level 4, when one or more of the aforementioned formative assessment levels are implemented on a schoolwide basis.

- *Instruction* is the means to a curricular end; *formative assessment* is a process intended to make a teacher's instructional means more effective.

- Level 1 formative assessment is a four-step process whereby the teacher (1) identifies assessment occasions, (2) selects assessment procedures, (3) establishes adjustment triggers, and (4) makes instructional adjustments.

CHAPTER

4

Students' Learning Tactic Adjustments

[Chapter Preview]

• What learning tactics are

• The roles of the students and the teacher in Level 2 formative assessment

• The three curricular clarifications the teacher must make

• The four steps of Level 2 formative assessment, a strategy for improving the caliber of learning tactics

FORMATIVE ASSESSMENT EXISTS FOR EXACTLY ONE REASON: to enhance students' learning. We've looked at one way it does this, through Level 1 formative assessment, which is the process of teachers adjusting their ongoing instructional activities based on assessment evidence. Now we turn to a second way formative assessment can enhance students' learning: through the process of students making their own evidence-based adjustments in the procedures they are using to try to learn what they're supposed to be learning.

If a teacher attempts to install Level 2 formative assessment in class, does this obligate the teacher to *also* employ Level 1 formative assessment? Well, although there's no formal require-ment for a teacher who's helping students adjust their learning tactics to also make adjustments in instruction, it would be truly *rare* for a teacher who's a Level 2 formative assessor not to also be a Level 1 formative assessor. Teachers who care enough about enhancing students' learning to help those students adjust their own learning tactics will almost certainly be teachers who care enough about enhancing students' learning to make war-ranted adjustments in their own instruction. Although Level 2 formative assessment can technically be present even in the absence of Level 1 formative assessment, such instances will be few and very far between.

A Look at Learning Tactics

A *learning tactic* is the way a student is trying to learn something. It can also be described as a learning procedure, learning tech-nique, or learning process. An example of a learning tactic would be the way a 6th grade student attempts to understand reading assignments in a social studies textbook by reading the assigned pages and then immediately preparing a written outline identify-ing the passage's most important points. The student's learning tactic is to "read the text and prepare a written outline." There are all sorts of other learning tactics this student could employ toward the goal of understanding a reading assignment, includ-ing preparing a written summary of the reading, discussing its main points with a parent, and delivering a simulated oral report about it in front of a mirror. Although the learning tactics are end-lessly variable, the function of Level 2 formative assessment is constant: to provide students with assessment-based evidence so they can decide whether their learning tactics are working or need to be adjusted.

Suppose, for example, that a major curricular aim of middle school English teacher Mr. Adams is to get his students to become skilled writers of descriptive essays. At the beginning of the school year, Mr. Adams explains to his students that he'll ask them to compose relatively brief descriptive essays every two or three weeks throughout the semester. Over the first two months of school, Sue Ames, one of his students, writes a draft of each assigned essay, revises it right away, and then submits it. This "instant revision," wherein Sue looks at her descriptive essay immediately after completing it and then goes back to change what she doesn't like, is her learning tactic.

Sue's first half-dozen essays, however, have been fairly weak. Mr. Adams's comment on five of those six essays is that they lack rich, evocative language. Recognizing her descriptive essays' shortcomings, Sue decides to adjust her learning tactic. Specifically, she will follow a classmate's advice to never revise a first-draft essay unless she's allowed it to "cool off" for at least 24 hours. In addition, Sue arranges to have another classmate, Melanie (whom Mr. Adams has praised for her skill in using evocative language), read and react to Sue's second-draft essay. In short, Sue intends to make two significant changes in the way she is trying to become a more skilled writer of descriptive essays. She plans to substantially shift the learning procedure she's been using because the assessment evidence embodied in her early essays suggests that her "instant revision" tactic is not effective.

New Game: New Rules, New Roles

Level 2 formative assessment consists of *student-determined* adjustments in learning tactics, not *teacher-dictated* adjustments the students are then supposed to make. The students' "starring role" is the fundamental difference between Level 1 and Level 2. Although teachers play an important part in Level 2 formative assessment, it is a *supporting role,* not a *decision-making* one. Here, the teacher's mission is to put students in a position to make assessment-based choices about whether they wish to alter the way they're trying to learn something. In a very real sense, then, the teacher needs to (1) structure the classroom situation so students can routinely secure assessment-elicited evidence regarding their progress and (2) encourage students to take personal responsibility for deciding whether and how to adjust any learning tactics in need of adjustment. The teacher, thus, becomes a stage setter and a facilitator, and the success of Level 2 formative assessment hinges on the degree to which the teacher transfers the lead decision-making role to students. It's not just that students are *permitted* to take personal responsibility for how they're trying to learn; they are *strongly encouraged* to do so.

For most teachers and students, Level 2 formative assessment represents a decisively new approach to instruction. Accordingly, teachers who choose to install Level 2 formative assessment in their classrooms must make a major commitment to readying their students to get the most out of this approach. Many students will need explicit instruction about what a "learning tactic" is and what latitude they will have in adjusting the learning tactics they ultimately decide to adopt. Many will also need to be convinced that the teacher really will allow them to be personally responsible for the selection and use of their own learning tactics and is genuinely serious about such an "abdication" of authority. With so much to communicate, the best way to begin is with a full-scale orientation.

Here is an illustrative orientation talk, presented by a high school history teacher during the first week of a brand new school year:

> Good morning students. This course in U.S. history is going to be organized in a way that most of you will find quite unusual. Not only am I going to do the best job I possibly can in getting you to acquire important skills and knowledge in U.S. history, but you are going to have a meaningful role yourselves in determining what you learn about U.S. history. Here's how this new approach is going to work. During the course, I will frequently collect assessment evidence from you regarding how well you are learning what you're supposed to be learning. Sometimes that assessment evidence will come from the typical sorts of paper-and-pencil tests you have taken in school for many years. In other cases, I'll be collecting assessment information in less formal, sometimes rather novel ways. This kind of evidence gathering is part of a process known as *formative assessment*, and its purpose is to help me improve the instruction you are receiving.

More specifically, the evidence I'll be getting from you by using formal and informal assessment has two purposes. First, it will help me determine whether I need to make adjustments in the instruction you're receiving. An important purpose of formative assessment is to help teachers decide what parts of their instruction, if any, need to be adjusted. But a second important purpose of formative assessment is that it will help you decide whether you need to make any adjustments in your learning tactics. A *learning tactic* is the name we'll use to describe the procedures you use when you're trying to learn something. Different students often use different learning tactics, and you'll get really good at identifying different sorts of learning tactics, then seeing if they work for you.

Throughout the course, I'll be identifying the most important historical skills and the most important bodies of historical knowledge you should be learning. I'll let you know not only the major skills and most important knowledge you ought to be learning but also what sorts of along-the-way subskills and knowledge you'll need in order to master those major skills and most important knowledge. I'll even help you keep track of your own progress in mastering those subskills and bodies of knowledge. Then, whenever I collect formative assessment evidence to help me decide whether to make instructional adjustments, I'll give each of you the same assessment evidence so that you can decide for yourself whether your personal learning tactics are working satisfactorily. You'll be deciding whether what you're doing is working for you and helping you master the material or if you need to change your approach. And if you decide that an adjustment would be a good idea, you'll be able to decide for yourself what that adjustment is going to be.

I'll try to help you figure out whether a learning tactic adjustment seems necessary, and I'll be offering some suggestions about the kinds of learning tactics that might work better. But, again, the ultimate decision regarding whether you change your learning tactics is up to *you,* not me.

I'll be posting a written summary of what I've just said on the class bulletin board later today, but I want you all to recognize that this approach to the study of U.S. history is definitely not "instruction as usual." By deciding whether you need to change your learning tactics based on the assessment evidence you'll be receiving, you can play a powerful, personal role in what you learn about U.S. history.

What *I* need to do is rely on formative assessment evidence to improve the quality of the instruction you receive; what *you* need to do is use the same formative assessment information to improve the effectiveness of your personal learning tactics. If we all do a good job in using the assessment evidence we'll be looking at, this will be a great class for all of us. Are there any questions?

The details of an orientation to Level 2 formative assessment will vary with the age of the students, the subject matter, and the procedural particulars the teacher has in mind. But it should always contain three key features, all of which are included in the foregoing sample: (1) why Level 2 formative assessment is being done, (2) how it will work, and (3) the importance of having students become personally responsible for their own learning tactic adjustments. It is also essential to let students know during the orientation that they will get the support they need.

In addition to this full-scale orientation, students will need ongoing training on how to arrive at sound decisions related to learning tactic adjustments. They will need to learn, for example, about the kinds of assessment-based evidence that will be available to them and how to make the best use of such evidence. Finally, students will need to become familiar with the full range of options they can employ when seeking different, more effective, learning tactics.

Clarifying Curricular Expectations

Because Level 2 formative assessment calls for students to play an especially active role in deciding whether their learning tactics are working properly, they must have a very clear idea not only of *what* they are supposed to learn but of *how* they are going to learn it. At various points during the school year, teachers must make certain their students understand three things:

1. The nature of the immediately upcoming curricular aim to be mastered—that is, the skill or body of knowledge students are supposed to learn;

2. The evaluative criteria to be employed in judging the quality of students' curricular-aim mastery; and

3. The chief building blocks involved in mastery—that is, the subskills and bodies of enabling knowledge students must master en route to attaining the target curricular aim.

When initiating a new unit of instruction, a teacher must always give students these three clarifications. Let's consider each on its own.

Clarification 1: The Nature of the Curricular Aim or Aims

As noted previously, a *curricular aim* describes the significant cognitive skill or body of knowledge students are supposed to learn. Curricular aims are sometimes referred to as *objectives*, *goals*, or *outcomes*. Fundamentally, whatever label you are inclined to hang on a curricular aim, it should articulate what students are supposed to know or be able to do at the conclusion of instruction.

Because, in Level 2 formative assessment, students play the dominant decision-making role in determining whether to adjust their learning tactics, it is *absolutely requisite* that students understand what curricular aims the teacher is promoting. At the outset of every new segment of instruction, whether the instruction is for a single lesson or for a multiweek unit, teachers need to describe the curricular aim or aims being pursued. I can recommend several helpful procedures for doing this.

Present the target curricular aim in language that students can understand. When talking about the target curricular aim with students, the teacher should be sure to rephrase it in a student-friendly form—one tailored to the particular students involved. To illustrate, consider the following target curricular aim from a middle school science course:

Original Curricular Aim
Students will be able to design and describe in writing an empirical, scientifically defensible research investigation suitable for identifying the relationships among two or more authentic variables.

Although science teachers might readily comprehend what is embodied in this curricular aim, its current phrasing is probably going to confuse many middle school students. Here is the same curricular aim again, rephrased in two different ways that students will be more likely to understand:

Rephrased Curricular Aim, Version 1
You will be asked to plan a research study intended to tell how two or more variables (things such as time or temperature) are related to one another. You'll need to describe your planned research study in writing. And you should incorporate the key scientific evidence-gathering procedures you will be learning about in class.

Rephrased Curricular Aim, Version 2
You will need to figure out how to organize a research study so that you can figure out how two or more variables (such as a person's weight and age) are related to each other. Then you will need to describe your planned study in writing.

A good way for a teacher to determine if a student-friendly version of a curricular aim accurately communicates the nature of that aim is to present it to several students and ask them to read it silently a few times. Next, the teacher might ask them to set the curricular aim aside and write a description, in their own words, of what the skill or body of knowledge being sought actually is. If different students independently produce similar descriptions of the curricular aim, it is likely the student-friendly version of the aim is appropriate. On the other hand, if different students' renditions of what's being sought by the curricular aim are quite diverse, it's likely that a reworking of the curricular aim's phrasing is necessary.

Curricular aims, in their original form or as specifically revised for students, must not function as Rorschach inkblots. Student-palatable versions of all significant curricular aims should be posted prominently in class during the time when instruction is focused on students' achievement of those curricular aims.

Explain the assessment procedures. Another good way for a teacher to help students better comprehend the nature of a curricular aim is to describe the way that mastery of that aim will be measured. Ideally, such descriptions will be accompanied by one or more sample items. To illustrate, for the foregoing curricular aims calling for students to design and describe a research design, the teacher could share an example of possible test items, such as this one:

> Focusing on measurable variables *in this classroom,* design a scientifically sound investigation that will provide evidence regarding the nature of the relationship between two of those variables. Describe your planned investigation in 1,000 words or less.

Teachers can and usually should explain to students *why* they've chosen a specific assessment technique to operationalize a curricular aim. This provides an excellent opportunity to enhance students' assessment literacy by describing various assessment options and, ultimately, why the one selected was best. Such explanations also provide an opportunity for teachers to communicate the substantial imprecision of educational measurement procedures and to indicate that multiple measurements typically yield more valid inferences about students' status related to a curricular aim than solo tests can.

Share extreme responses. There is one additional classification procedure that often helps students get a better fix on the nature of a target curricular aim, and it is the teacher's use of a pair of student responses, one of them very good and one of them very poor. (Remember, because most of the target curricular aims to be addressed as part of the formative assessment process will be cognitive skills rather than knowledge acquisition, and because such cognitive skills are typically assessed using constructed-response rather than selected-response assessment, many formative assessment activities culminate in a student being able to generate an original response from scratch.) The teacher either uses students' responses from previous classes or, if necessary, creates mock responses: one really strong response and one really weak response. (In the latter circumstance, the teacher should tell students that these are teacher-generated examples, not actual student responses.) There's no need at this early point to go into the subtleties that might distinguish a slightly weaker from a slightly stronger response. The purpose of this good-exemplar-versus-bad-exemplar activity is to allow students to contrast two extremely different qualities of students' responses.

Taken together, these clarification procedures should enable most students to acquire a reasonably solid understanding of what they will be working toward.

Clarification 2: The Evaluative Criteria

It's one thing for students to understand what the nature of a curricular aim is; it's quite another for them to know how they are to display mastery of that aim. The second way a teacher can clarify a curricular expectation is to help students understand the *evaluative criteria* to be employed when determining the quality of their performances.

To illustrate, suppose a speech teacher is trying to get her students to be skilled in making three-minute impromptu speeches to classmates. The teacher has decided to use the following evaluative criteria to determine the quality of these impromptu speeches: (1) organization, (2) content, (3) eye contact, and (4) avoidance of distracting mannerisms. To help students understand what each of these four evaluative criteria signifies, the teacher could provide "good" and "bad" examples of each. For instance, the speech teacher might show students a brief video sequence of a well-organized impromptu speech and contrast it with another video of an impromptu presentation where no organization can be discerned. Because, in Level 2 formative assessment, students play the dominant decision-making role in determining whether to adjust their learning tactics, it is *absolutely requisite* that students understand the evaluative criteria by which the quality of their performances will subsequently be judged. How can students make decisions about the effectiveness of their progress in mastering a particular curricular outcome if they don't know the factors by which their performance is to be evaluated?

Ideally, this clarification of the relevant evaluative criteria can be communicated to students in the form of a *rubric*, a scoring guide presented to students at the outset of instruction. Rubrics clarify how to appraise a student's performances, and they can be remarkably useful in helping students understand the nature of the curricular aim being sought. But not all rubrics are created equal. Do not assume that any collection of evaluative criteria automatically becomes a first-rate rubric. Well-formed rubrics, for instance, those containing a modest number of well-described evaluative criteria, help students understand what they are supposed to be learning. Weak rubrics, those with too many ill-defined evaluative criteria, usually are of little help to students or to the teacher. If you intend to use rubrics as a key way of clarifying curricular expectations, be sure to do your homework so that you can tell the righteous rubrics from the repugnant ones. And if you have a hankering to learn more about the difference between wretched and rapturous rubrics, you might take a peek at two other books of mine, in which I spend more time wrestling with rubric quality (Popham, 2003, 2008).

Clarification 3: The Building Blocks

The last of three important clarifications teachers must supply to students is to lay out the sequence of subskills and bodies of enabling knowledge identified in the learning progression underlying the target curricular aim in question.

The reason it is so crucial for the teacher to identify the en route building blocks, and the order in which they are to be learned, is that students will typically be making learning tactic adjustment decisions associated with each of those building blocks. Therefore, they must understand, at least in general terms, what these building blocks are, namely, what they must master en route to their mastery of the target curricular aim. How can students make decisions about the effectiveness of their learning tactics with regard to the learning progression's building blocks if they don't know what those building blocks are?

What makes this clarification task a little more challenging is that, at the start of a unit or lesson, students don't yet know much about the content and the target curricular aim, let alone its subskills and enabling knowledge. When a teacher explains those building blocks in advance, these explanations aren't likely to be very meaningful to students or make much of an impression. As instruction progresses, and students become more familiar with the content, the teacher will typically have an easier time of isolating and describing each of the learning progression's building blocks. More importantly, students will have an easier time grasping their meaning. At the outset of a unit or lesson, when expectation-clarification is taking place, it's usually sufficient to give a very general overview of the sequence of building blocks. I recommend creating a poster-sized diagram of the learning progression to display on a classroom bulletin board and distributing a graphic or verbal representation of the learning progression to all students as soon as sensible.

What students really need to recognize at this time is that the teacher will be collecting assessment evidence related to each of the learning progression's building blocks—these specific subskills and these particular bodies of enabling knowledge—for the purpose of making instructional adjustments. The teacher will channel this assessment evidence to them too, so that they may judge whether or not they need to try a new learning tactic.

One Mission, Four Analogous Activities

You'll remember that Level 1 formative assessment revolves around the teacher's four-step operation of (1) identifying adjustment occasions, (2) selecting assessments, (3) establishing adjustment triggers, and (4) making instructional adjustments. In Level 2 assessment, students engage in an analogous four-step procedure, shown in Figure 4.1.

Figure 4.1 | Students' Level 2 Steps

Step 1: Consider adjustment occasions.
The student considers teacher recommendations regarding when during an instructional sequence learning tactic adjustment decisions might best be made.

Step 2: Consider assessments.
The student considers teacher-identified potential assessment procedures that can contribute to learning tactic adjustment decisions.

Step 3: Consider adjustment triggers.
The student considers teacher-identified potential levels of student performance that indicate learning tactic adjustments are warranted.

Step 4: Consider and adjust learning tactics.
The student considers teacher-proposed learning tactic adjustments to improve the effectiveness of those tactics and decides on the adjustment to make.

Although the teacher's role is chiefly *assistive*, it is still critical, focused on offering students suggestions on how to proceed through the four-step process and arrive at defensible decisions about whether to adjust learning tactics. Note that in each of these steps, the student is asked to consider the teacher's suggestion, but the decision, ultimately, is the student's. It's time now to consider each step in more detail.

Step 1: Students Consider Adjustment Occasions

We know that the teacher initiates Level 2 formative assessment by clarifying to students the curricular expectations they face: the nature of the target curricular aim itself, the evaluative criteria by which performance will be judged, and the building blocks represented in the learning progression underlying the specific curricular aim. Immediately after doing so, the teacher must help students identify the most likely occasions when they can make evidence-based decisions about whether to adjust their learning tactics.

Here, in Step 1, the teacher spells out for students the specific occasions when there will be assessment evidence available for consideration. Typically, such occasions arise in connection with the teacher's assessments linked to students' building-block mastery. The same data from building-block assessments that teachers must use to guide decisions about possible instructional adjustments should inform students' decisions about possible learning tactic adjustments. Accordingly, teachers need to let their students know that during an instructional sequence, such as a four-week unit dealing with a particular curricular aim (perhaps how to summarize effectively), students will be given a certain number of assessment results, collected formally or informally, that will show their status with respect to mastery of each building block in the learning progression. After this information is supplied to them, their role is to use it to judge the appropriateness of their current learning tactics. Is what they're doing working, or would it be wise to try something else?

Having promised to get such building-block assessment information to students, a Level 2 formative assessment teacher must deliver this information to students as soon as possible after assessing those students. Once students have the data, however, it should remain each student's individual choice as to whether to modify or stick with current learning tactics.

Step 2: Students Consider Assessment Procedures

The chief thrust of this second step of Level 2 formative assessment is for the teacher to take on the serious responsibility of continually apprising students of formal and informal assessment activities that might illuminate students' decisions about the adequacy of their current learning tactics. Granting that most teachers will be devoting more attention to doing a crackerjack instructional job than to abetting students in a quest for optimally effective learning tactics, teachers who choose to implement Level 2 formative assessment must be sure they make a serious commitment to helping their students obtain the assessment-based information those students need in order to decide whether to retain or alter their learning tactics. Without such assessment evidence, students simply can't make informed decisions about how they're trying to learn something, and Level 2 formative assessment becomes a charade.

Rare are the students who are inclined to whip-up tests on their own volition. During any sort of Level 2 formative assessment, the actual assessment approaches typically come from teachers, not students. So, when a teacher suggests to students what sorts of evidence-gathering assessments they should consider using, realism suggests that most of those assessments will be teacher-generated assessment procedures.

Focus on building-block assessments. Because the teacher will be carrying out assessments based on each of a learning progression's building blocks, those assessments will provide students with evidence they can use to arrive at independent judgments of how well they have mastered each of the learning progression's building blocks. In the midst of an extended sequence of instruction, teachers may also decide they need to collect evidence of students' status with respect to an aspect of a building block not originally identified as especially important. Results of these sorts of unforeseen assessments, such as along-the-way quizzes or brief-essay exams, should also be made available to students to inform their decisions about learning tactic adjustments.

Supplement with optional assessments. In an optimal educational world, students would also have access to a set of optional, "choose-to-use" assessments, complete with answer keys to facilitate self-scoring. These allow students, if they wish, to periodically gauge their own mastery of all building blocks and the target curricular aim itself. By making such optional assessments available, a teacher increases the likelihood that students can find out how well they are learning the stuff they are supposed to be learning. Teachers committed to formative assessment might consider establishing a set of tests tailored to a particular curricular aim and its associated building blocks and then expanding this set over the years. Making these tests (and their answer keys) available to students as part of the formative assessment process gives students yet another way of determining how satisfactorily they are progressing and whether they should adjust the learning tactics they've been employing.

Consider peer assessment. Another potentially powerful way for students to obtain assessment-based evidence regarding their progress is to employ peer assessment. Peer assessment can take many forms, but its central feature is that students play an important part in assessing each other. In some applications of peer assessment, classmates simply use an established rubric to evaluate each others' responses; the peer assessors are, in reality, only peer-scorers. In other variations of peer assessment, students who have already mastered the curricular aim being sought actually generate their own ways of assessing other students' status with respect to that curricular aim. They might, for example, volunteer to be members of a "Testing Team" for different segments of instruction. Testing Team members agree to come up with one or more assessment procedures (oral or in writing) that can be used with other students who opt to participate. When using this kind of peer evaluation, it's a good idea to encourage Testing Team members to exchange ideas about how to measure their classmates' status with regard to the curricular aim or a specific building block. Such conversations typically improve the quality of student-generated assessment techniques.

WHITEBOARDS AND WHITE (MEANING GOOD) NOISE

Kathy Bartley, a veteran education with 20 years of experience, teaches chemistry and physics at Highland High School in Highland, Indiana. Although many educators think of erasable whiteboards as a classroom tool more suitable for elementary students than for secondary ones, a decade's worth of experience tells Kathy otherwise.

"I've been using whiteboards as a form of assessment for the past 10 years," she says. "Not only do I find them an excellent way to tell if students understand a concept, but my students do too. They beg me to use whiteboards because they find out for themselves if they understand the concepts being covered and where they need to study more."

Kathy typically uses whiteboards before a quiz or test. With students working in self-selected pairs, she posts a set of problems for all to see—problems from a worksheet, from the textbook or that she has created—about 10 per concept she wants to cover. The partners work through each problem on their whiteboard and then turn it to Kathy to display their response. If it is correct, she gives them the go-ahead to move to the next problem; if it is not, she tells them to try again, sometimes calling attention to faulty reasoning or offering a hint to put them on the right track.

"What is so nice about these whiteboard activities is the noise and excitement in the room," Kathy says. "It is good noise. Students are actually talking about the problems and working hard at getting them right. As the students work in pairs, there are rarely slackers; they 'get on' each other to solve the problems properly and efficiently."

She adds, "In addition to the science course I teach now, I have taught different math classes and students in basic-level courses to advanced-placement ones. Students in all these classes love whiteboard activities. And I love them too because they allow me to make adjustments in my lessons based on how the majority of students perform. I can reteach if I feel I should, or I can give students a paper-and-pencil test the following day. And my students always know exactly what to expect. This is clearly a win–win situation for everyone."

One of the most difficult challenges facing peer assessors is the question of how to relay assessment results to classmates in a constructive manner. It is usually necessary for the teacher to spend some extra time with peer assessors so they can become more skilled in transmitting assessment results in way that preserves the dignity of the classmate being assessed and also presents the assessment information in a fashion that will help the classmate decide whether an adjustment in learning tactics is warranted.

A teacher who wishes to incorporate a good deal of peer assessment into Level 2 formative assessment must give careful thought to the logistics of how this procedure is going to work and then plan accordingly. If, for instance, there will be a Testing Team for each major curricular aim being taught, it's important to come up with a sensible set of procedures whereby students who need assessment assistance from a member of the Testing Team can secure such assistance without disrupting other ongoing classroom activities.

Check for (and then check out) state or district computer-based assessments. As I was taking a final look at the edited version of this book, I learned that just the day before the Kansas Department of Education had released on its Web site a series of mathematics assessments developed by the University of Kansas for use by the state's teachers and students. This very sophisticated set of materials, some patently suitable for use as part of the formative assessment process, made me realize that in the near future it is likely that many other states, and school districts as well, will make online assessment materials available. Some of these assessment materials may be highly suitable for use by students as part of a Level 2 approach to formative assessment. The Kansas assessment materials, all of which are based on that state's official curricular aims, would be suitable as a final rehearsal assessment, that is, an exam to help students discover if their mastery of a target curricular aim is satisfactory. (At the moment, the Kansas computer-based assessment materials do not measure students' status with respect to those en route building blocks that might constitute a learning progression leading toward a target curricular aim. However, in the future, those assessment materials might do precisely this.)

In the years ahead, computer-based assessment instruments are likely to serve as a rich source of assessment options available to both teachers and students. Teachers should be on the lookout for such measurement materials but also be sure to judge the relevance of any such materials for their particular instructional requirements. Merely because an assessment tool travels to you through the ether does not mean that you must use it.

Support students' assessment literacy. Because Level 2 formative assessment calls for students to rely on assessment-produced evidence regarding their attainment of various skills, subskills, and bodies of knowledge, this second step in the process provides teachers with a marvelous opportunity to familiarize students with cornerstone truths about educational assessment itself. For instance, because students are frequently urged to arrive at their own decisions regarding mastery of a learning progression's building blocks, those students really need to understand how a set of test results can allow someone (a teacher *or* a student) to arrive at an accurate score-based inference about a student's status regarding the skill, subskill, or body of knowledge being measured. This is when assessment *validity* comes galloping onstage. Teachers can help students understand it is a test-based *inference* that's valid or invalid, not a test itself. Students can learn what it is to make a "false-positive" or a "false-negative" inference about a student's status. They need to learn the basics of educational assessment simply because Level 2 formative assessment requires them to make a substantial number of assessment-based decisions.

Leave grades out of it. While on the topic of assessments, it should be recalled that *none* of the assessments functioning as part of the formative assessment process ought to be graded. The function of formative assessment's evidence gathering is to help teachers (in Level 1) and students (in Level 2) make decisions intended to enhance students' learning. Therefore, teachers should build and use assessments to gather evidence of what it is that students know and can do, not to compare students' performances with one another. Similarly, students should complete assessments not with the intention of earning high grades, but rather, with the hope of securing an accurate idea about what they know and don't know.

If certain tests are required for grade-giving purposes, as they are in many settings, students' scores on these tests should not be part of the formative assessment process, and teachers should inform students of this fact well in advance.

Step 3: Students Consider Adjustment Triggers

Step 3 in Level 2 formative assessment calls for the teacher to supply students with guidance about what level of performance on particular assessments would indicate the need to make a learning tactic adjustment. Note that the teacher should provide this guidance for each assessment, because different assessments attempt to measure different things and may vary in level of difficulty. Given this variability, it would be absurd for a teacher to issue a blanket pronouncement such as, "Consider adjusting your learning tactics if your assessment performance ever falls below 80 percent correct."

This third step also provides a great opportunity for a teacher to familiarize students not only with the imprecision of standards-setting for purposes of deciding whether to adjust a learning tactic but also with the imprecision of standards setting in general. When policymakers attempt to arrive at high-stakes tests' "cut scores," which differentiate "proficient" performance from "advanced" performance, there is often a remarkable amount of arbitrariness involved. Even though the standards-setters are usually well trained and thoughtful and try to exercise their very best judgment, some degree of judgmental imprecision is always present.

With the inherent frailty of standards-setting duly acknowledged, there's still little question that a teacher possesses far more experience than students do when it comes to determining the cut scores in formative assessment—the measure of *how well* a student needs to have mastered an en route building block in order to subsequently master the target curricular aim itself.

As a consequence, teachers have a responsibility to share their opinions about suggested adjustment triggers with students.

Remembering that Level 2 formative assessment must be a student-determined enterprise, if a student chooses to establish trigger levels other than those the teacher suggests, that's the way a Level 2 teacher must leave it. The teacher should simply note the students' choices and check in periodically to see if those choices are serving the students well. After students have used their chosen performance level in arriving at adjust-or-not decisions about learning tactics, it is certainly acceptable for a teacher to try to help students arrive at a level that's more defensible. For example, suppose several students select a 100-percent-correct adjustment trigger, meaning that they plan to alter learning tactics in response to anything but a perfect score. Then the teacher might sensibly suggest that a performance level of perfection is almost certain to result in too many false negatives, committing students to changing their learning tactics even though those tactics may have been very effective, if not quite effective enough to boost performances to a totally flaw-free level. The teacher should point out that a more realistic adjustment trigger would help prevent this kind of mistake

Step 4: Students Consider and Adjust Learning Tactics

In the final step of Level 2 formative assessment, a teacher should focus on helping students understand what kinds of learning tactic adjustments might prove most beneficial. It's also another chance for teachers to familiarize students with several key principles of assessment and also with important principles of learning—principles that, if incorporated properly, could transform an ineffectual learning tactic into one that works fabulously.

To help students decide how to adjust their learning tactics, teachers do need to discover what learning tactics their students are currently using. Because tactics will differ for different curricular aims, it makes sense for a teacher to spend a few moments getting students to describe the learning tactics they're using in an attempt to master a particular curricular aim or building block. By spending several minutes of a class discussion on this topic, the teacher can often comment on the likely effectiveness of certain student-described learning tactics and then suggest possible ways that those tactics might be strengthened. For instance, because sufficient "engaged time on task" is so important for the success of most learning tactics, teachers might suggest that the majority of approaches students adopt should be sure to include ample opportunities for a student to successfully practice whatever skill or knowledge a building block or curricular aim calls for.

I've said it throughout our consideration of Level 2 formative assessment, and I'll say it again now: The role of the teacher here is to set forth suggestions so students will be able to arrive at better choices. As always, if students choose not to adopt the teacher's suggestions regarding learning tactics, then the teacher simply swallows hard and moves forward. This doesn't mean the teacher is "writing off" such students; the teacher will still work at helping them learn what they should. But if Level 2 formative assessment is going to be genuine rather than phony, it must be *students* who assume a meaningful chunk of the responsibility for their own learning. The only way they will become good at doing this is if their teacher nurtures such responsibility at every step of the process but does not take over what must, in the final analysis, be the individual student's decision. It's another reminder that the most challenging aspect of this application of formative assessment is for a teacher to accept the role of facilitator rather than that of decision maker. But it can be worth the effort because of the insights students gain and the habits they develop in terms of setting standards for themselves, examining their practices, and making adjustments in how they try to learn things. This kind of outcome is likely to be far more significant and long-lasting than mastery of any particular curricular aim set forth in a set of state academic standards.

SUPER-SUCCINCT SUMMARY

- In Level 2 formative assessment, teachers provide students with assessment evidence so that students can decide whether to adjust the learning tactics they are currently using in an effort to master a particular curricular aim. The teacher's role is to facilitate and suggest, not to decide.

- Before implementing Level 2 formative assessment, the teacher must clarify curricular expectations for students to help them make their adjustment decisions with greater accuracy. Such curricular clarification includes providing students with (1) the curricular aim being pursued, rephrased as necessary to enhance student comprehension; (2) the evaluative criteria by which students can judge the quality of their performances; and (3) at least a rudimentary idea of the sequence of building blocks to be mastered en route to mastering the target curricular aim.

- The four central steps of Level 2 formative assessment occur when students consider teacher-suggested (1) adjustment occasions, (2) assessment procedures, (3) adjustment triggers, and (4) decide on teacher-suggested learning tactic adjustments.

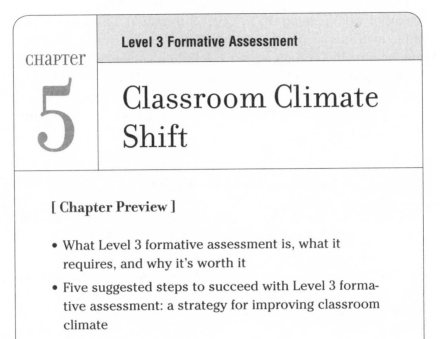

CHAPTER

5

Classroom Climate Shift

[Chapter Preview]

- What Level 3 formative assessment is, what it requires, and why it's worth it
- Five suggested steps to succeed with Level 3 formative assessment: a strategy for improving classroom climate

SO FAR, OUR FOCUS HAS BEEN ON FORMATIVE ASSESSMENT'S *adjustments*. More specifically, we have considered adjustments teachers make in their instructional procedures (Level 1 formative assessment) and adjustments students make in their learning tactics (Level 2 formative assessment). These sorts of adjustments, while requiring some effort to carry out successfully, are relatively easy to understand. In this chapter, we will be dealing with a decisively different magnitude of adjustment: how teachers can fundamentally adjust the total climate of their classrooms.

If you prefer to think of Level 3 formative assessment as changing a classroom's *culture* or its *atmosphere*, this is perfectly acceptable. And if you choose to get a little ritzy, you might even think of what's going on in Level 3 formative assessment as a shift in a classroom's *zeitgeist*. That German word, best pronounced with Teutonic gusto, refers to a society's "spirit of the times." But irrespective of the label you plaster on it, Level 3 formative assessment requires a pervasive change in the way *students and teachers* think about what should go on in their classroom.

A Shift . . . but *From* What *To* What?

Whenever anyone contemplates making a major shift, it's only natural to wonder about the nature of that shift. Because Level 3 formative assessment describes a fundamental change in a classroom's climate, it makes sense to identify precisely what kind of shift is involved. Actually, Level 3 formative assessment calls for a fundamental change in three dimensions of the classroom: *learning expectations*, *responsibility for learning*, and *the perceived role of classroom assessment*. Figure 5.1 details the nature of these three changes. As you can see, in Level 3 formative assessment, both teachers and students end up altering their perceptions about what goes on in class.

Moreover, these new ways of thinking will typically kick off changes in classroom activities, especially those associated with instruction and classroom assessment. It would not be a misrepresentation to characterize Level 3 formative assessment as a shift from a *traditional classroom climate*, the kind of classroom that most of today's adults experienced as children, toward a more modern, *assessment-informed classroom climate*. If you were to spend 30 minutes in the classroom of a teacher who has successfully implemented Level 3 formative assessment, you'd quickly discern some fundamental differences in both expectation and attitude:

Figure 5.1	The Key Classroom Climate Shifts in Level 3 Formative Assessment

	From		To
Learning Expectations	Substantial learning will occur for motivated students who possess adequate academic aptitude.	→	Substantial learning will occur for all students, irrespective of their academic aptitude.
Responsibility for Learning	The teacher, as prime instructional mover, is chiefly responsible for students' learning.	→	Students assume meaningful responsibility for their own learning and the learning of their classmates.
Role of Classroom Assessment	Formal tests generate data for comparing students and assigning grades.	→	Formal and informal assessments generate data for informing adjustments to the teacher's instruction and the students' learning tactics.

• Teachers are focused on helping students learn as much as possible, as rapidly as possible, and students share this preoccupation;

• There is a spirit of collaboration, not competitiveness. Students see themselves as instructional partners who have a significant responsibility for making sure learning takes place; and

• Students express genuine concern about the learning progress that *other* students are making.

What supports this climate shift? It's the fact that, in a Level 3 classroom, formal and informal assessments routinely supply the evidence the teacher and students need to make appropriate learning-related decisions.

The First Two Prerequisites: Level 1 and Level 2 Formative Assessment

It should be apparent that Level 3 formative assessment only makes sense if a teacher has also installed Levels 1 and 2 formative assessment. But, as you have surely seen, Level 3 formative assessment clearly moves *beyond* those first two levels. Accomplishing a classroom climate shift requires a teacher to carry out several activities deliberately aimed at bringing about such a fundamental change in classroom culture. These sorts of activities are not particularly time consuming, but they are potent ways of making Level 3 formative assessment a reality. We'll consider the nature of those activities shortly.

While we're speaking of time, though, when does it make sense, timing-wise, for a teacher to try to install Level 3 formative assessment? If a teacher were intent on creating a totally different learning atmosphere in his or her classroom, should that action be undertaken *after* the teacher has implemented Level 1 and Level 2 formative assessment, as the next in a series of incremental steps? Or should all three levels of formative assessment be initiated simultaneously? This is an important procedural question akin to deciding the arrangement of a learning progression's building blocks. As was the case with the building-block issue, there's no always-correct answer to this key question. And, as is usually true when trying to solve a classroom instructional puzzle, it depends chiefly on the teacher.

Some teachers are incrementalists who will be more comfortable in adopting a one-step-at-a-time approach to classroom change. They may prefer to spend a few weeks getting Level 1 formative assessment up and running, then a few weeks establishing Level 2 formative assessment, and only at that point move to the installation of Level 3. At each new phase of this three-phase strategy, the teacher can explain to students what's taking place. These along-the-way explanations help to ensure that when the teacher finally moves to Level 3 formative assessment, the students will understand its comprehensive nature. At that point, the teacher's message to the students will be along these lines:

> OK, you've seen how we've moved through the *I-adjust-my-instruction* and *you-adjust-your-learning-tactics* phases of formative assessment. Now it's time to blend those two phases together so that we, together, can totally transform how we approach learning in this class.

Other teachers will not have the patience that incrementalism requires. Rather than installing Level 1, then Level 2, and then Level 3 formative assessment, they'd rather get everything under way immediately and put all three levels into play at once. Such an all-at-once implementation of the three formative-assessment levels might find a teacher saying something such as this:

> Boys and girls, this class will be operated in a way that is probably going to be very different from the way you've been taught in the past. I'll be describing this approach in more detail later, but you'll find that we're going to be using assessment evidence—the evidence obtained from how you perform on classroom quizzes and a number of other informal sorts of tests—to improve how well you learn. I'm going to use this assessment evidence to adjust how I'm teaching you. And I'd like you to use that assessment evidence to adjust the ways you're trying to learn things. Overall, we're going to work every day to help each other learn just as much as we possibly can learn. We're going to do this together, and we're going to start doing so this very minute!

There is no body of evidence bearing on the question of whether a teacher who sets out to install Level 3 formative assessment ought to do it only after students become accustomed to Levels 1 and 2, or whether it's better to implement all three levels at once. Thus, it really does boil down to an individual teacher's preference.

The Second Two Prerequisites: Commitment and Resilience

Teachers who want to change the basic climate of their classroom won't accomplish that change simply by announcing to students there will be a new set of ground rules to follow. Setting out to fundamentally alter the climate of a classroom is a nontrivial undertaking, and teachers who decide to install Level 3 formative assessment should be committed to the goal and prepared to devote substantial energy to its monitoring and upkeep, at least until the new repertoire of teacher behaviors and student behaviors is well established and becomes routine. And because teachers are unlikely to get Level 3 formative assessment exactly right the first time around, teachers working at this level of formative assessment need to be resilient. If a planned procedure that seemed likely to work turns out *not* to contribute to the climate sought in a Level 3 classroom, the teacher should be ready to modify this less-than-lustrous procedure promptly. In a very real sense, teachers who wish to install Level 3 formative assessment need to keep their eye on the target, but in this instance it is a three-segment target, such as the one depicted in Figure 5.2, identifying the dimensions key to a meaningful classroom climate shift:

1. *Learning expectations.* Do all assignments, activities, and assessments reflect the teacher's belief that all students will master all curricular aims? Do students' behavior and actions suggest that they believe success is within their grasp?

2. *Responsibility for learning.* Do assignments, activities, and assessments place significant responsibility for learning on students, as individuals and as members of a community of learners? Do the students' actions and behavior show that they're assuming meaningful responsibility for their own success and the success of their classmates?

3. *The role of classroom assessment.* Is classroom assessment consistently employed to generate evidence of learning with the goal of informing teacher and student adjustments? Do both students and the teacher see it as the means to improve learning rather than the means for ranking and comparing students?

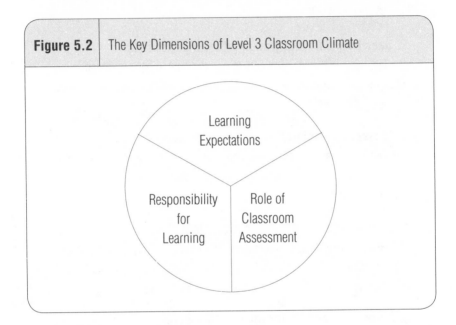

Figure 5.2 | The Key Dimensions of Level 3 Classroom Climate

Suggested Steps for Level 3 Success

Assuming a teacher is firmly committed to making Level 3 formative assessment fly, how does that teacher go about establishing a Level 3 classroom? I have five activities to recommend, listed in Figure 5.3. Only the first of these steps is absolutely mandatory, and the rest need not be carried out in the presented order, but their adoption will increase the probability of Level 3's success. Indeed, other than Step 1, which I regard as imperative, teachers may come up with their own, better ways of reinforcing a shift in thinking about learning expectations, responsibility for learning, and the role of classroom assessment. Go with whatever works, but as a starting point, consider the steps I recommend.

Figure 5.3	Teachers' Suggested Steps for Establishing Level 3 Formative Assessment

1. Distribute classroom climate guidelines.

The teacher informs students of the ground rules that everyone (students and the teacher) will follow.

2. Seek trust constantly and nurture it seriously.

The teacher consistently attempts to get students to have confidence in what, for many of them, will be a new way of thinking about both instruction and assessment.

3. Model and reinforce appropriate conduct.

The teacher behaves in a manner consonant with the kind of class atmosphere being sought and is always on the lookout for suitable student actions to reinforce.

4. Solicit students' advice on classroom climate.

The teacher provides mechanisms for students to supply advice regarding the classroom's climate and frequently invites students to offer such advice.

5. Assess students' relevant affective status.

The teacher periodically assesses students' status with respect to the affective variables most relevant to the kind of classroom atmosphere being promoted.

Step 1: Distribute Classroom Climate Guidelines

Because the kind of classroom conduct sought in Level 3 formative assessment will be quite unusual for most students, this first activity is more of a must than a suggestion. Both orally and in writing, a teacher needs to let students know the nature of what's going on in class.

The specifics of such guidelines will vary, depending on the ages of the students involved and the teacher's own procedural preferences. Here is an illustration of what a solid set of class-room climate guidelines would look like, as delivered by fictional high school English teacher Lee Evans during the first class session of a new school year.

After welcoming students to 9th grade English and explaining the basic functions and terminology of Level 1 and Level 2 formative assessment, Lee spends several moments discussing the three key dimensions of classroom climate that Level 3 assessment will change, namely, learning expectations, responsibility for learning, and the role of classroom assessment. Using a flip chart, he provides a display akin to the one in Figure 5.1, showing the desired from/to shift in each of these three dimensions. Lee first describes each dimension and then explains the sort of shift he hopes will take place. After answering students' questions about the nature of these dimensions, he continues like this:

> Because the whole point of formative assessment is to improve how well you're learning, I hope we'll all soon see a genuine shift in the atmosphere of our class. Using all sorts of assessment-based evidence about your individual progress, we can jointly come up with ways that all of you will learn what you need to learn. You won't be competing against one another because each of you will be using the formative assessment process to make real progress.
>
> I'm asking each of you to work with me to make this a remarkably effective course, a course in which we join together to get wonderful learning results for everyone. In other words, I hope you'll personally take on some of the responsibility for learning. As the school year gets under way, I'll show you a number of ways you can take an active part in becoming responsible for what's learned in class.
>
> Finally, I want you to realize that, in this course, educational assessment is going to function very differently than it usually does. The purpose of assessment in our course is not to give grades. Instead, we'll use a whole collection of informal assessment procedures, such as when you respond on whiteboards during in-class quizzes and when you complete tests anonymously, to help me decide when to adjust instruction and to help you decide when to adjust your own learning tactics. Assessment is going to become the evidence-producing tool that helps all of us figure out what to do next. We're going to base our efforts to promote your mastery of 9th grade English on lots of assessment evidence, which we'll collect from you during the course. And, because we're going to be doing this together, and because all of you will be learning, there's going to

be a genuinely different learning climate in our course. It's really going to be exciting. So, let's get started!

Obviously, teachers need to do more than describe classroom climate guidelines only once and post them on the bulletin board. Students will need help, especially at the outset, figuring out what's expected in a classroom where formative assessment engenders a dramatically different climate for learning.

Step 2: Seek Trust Constantly and Nurture It Seriously

This approach to classroom instruction is definitely a different kind of game for both teachers and students. Early on and all the way throughout any instruction that goes on, teachers need to work hard at gaining the trust of their students with respect to the chief elements of full-blown formative assessment:

• Students need to believe the teacher is invested in having all students succeed—not just those who are the "best" students.

• Students need to believe the teacher is using formative assessment's test results *exclusively* for improved student learning—*not* for allocating grades and *not* for determining who is a "smart" or "good" student and who is not.

• Students need to believe the teacher is genuinely seeking their collaboration in assuming responsibility for their own learning.

In general, then, students must believe their teacher really wants to establish a dramatically different classroom climate. Yes, being a Level 3 teacher comes with numerous trust-enhancement obligations, but unless students really do trust in their teacher's commitment to this atypical instructional approach, Level 3 formative assessment will probably fizzle.

Like most well-sharpened swords, trust cuts both ways. This is definitely the case here. Although a teacher needs to *continually* work at gaining students' trust, some of the trust-promotion needs to come from students as well. If students regard a Level 3 classroom as one in which it is easier to elude personal responsibility and then go on to do just that, the potential benefits of formative assessment will be lost to them and to their classmates. If teachers suspect they're being conned by a set of self-serving students, they might understandably decide to return to a more conventional approach to instruction—an approach that is likely to instructionally shortchange at least some members of the class. The teacher's best bet here is to clarify for students how a classroom climate shift will benefit them and why it is worthy of their trust.

Step 3: Model and Reinforce Appropriate Conduct

It's important for teachers to explain and model the kinds of collaborative, learning-focused behavior called for in Level 3 formative assessment and to show students how to conduct themselves in this unfamiliar sort of classroom setting. For example, teachers may need to set up role-play scenarios wherein they and the students deliberately model appropriate behavior in respect to peer-assessment or peer-learning activities.

Similarly, Level 3 teachers need to be particularly attentive to the interpersonal and individual behaviors of their students and be on the lookout to reinforce conduct that meshes with the classroom climate aspirations inherent in Level 3 formative assessment. Examples of this might be when a student tries to help a classmate who's clearly confused about a task or when students encourage one another to master a key building block. When students display appropriate behaviors, the teacher can provide the appropriate praise and recognition, through public acknowledgment or personal conversation.

Step 4: Solicit Students' Advice on Classroom Climate

If students are being asked to assume at least some responsibility for learning, then they should also be encouraged to help shape the climate that's emerging. Level 3 teachers should periodically urge students to offer suggestions on how to "make it better." Because students are sometimes shy about supplying this kind of advice to their teacher in a face-to-face way, it is a good idea to use a suggestion box to facilitate anonymous recommendations for classroom climate improvement. Teachers should check the suggestion box routinely and then, in the spirit of trust-promotion, describe the reasoning behind any classroom changes stemming from students' suggestions. It might sound something like this:

> Someone in the class has suggested that we try having an end-of-the-week checkup quiz every Friday so that everyone can see how they're doing. As usual, these quizzes would not be graded. This seems like an excellent idea. I think one way to make this happen might be to have a group of volunteer "test-writers" help me create these quizzes. What do you think?

What the use of a suggestion box or similar feedback mechanisms should convey is the teacher's willingness to thoughtfully consider students' recommendations regarding classroom climate or, more generally, students' advice regarding any aspect of instruction.

Step 5: Assess Students' Relevant Affective Status

Climate, whether it describes what goes on in a classroom or refers to the weather that surrounds us, is tough to get a handle on. As teachers try to bring about a Level 3 classroom climate shift, they often benefit from additional ways to monitor what's taking place, sometimes unseen, before their very eyes. An anonymously completed affective inventory focused on classroom climate, administered every month or two, can supply teachers with useful insights regarding students' perceptions of the classroom climate and the progress of the hoped-for Level 3 shift. The reason I stipulate this inventory should be completed anonymously is that anonymous inventories guarantee a teacher will make a *group-focused* inference about students' classroom climate sentiments. It's the entire class's overall affective status the teacher is trying to get a fix on, not the perceptions of individual students.

Although step-by-step procedures for creating affective assessment inventories are available from other sources (for example, Popham, 2006, 2008), the example of a classroom

CLASSROOM ZEITGEIST AND TRUE/FALSE TESTS

It's impossible to measure the zeitgeist of a classroom using a true/false test—even one that's been translated into German. For this particularly complex challenge, you need an especially nimble assessment tool, and that's where affective inventories come in.

I've been advocating the use of affective assessments for more than 40 years because I believe affective variables are educationally important. Educators may talk to each other about focusing on students' attitudes, interests, and values, but unless we assess these variables, meaningful attention to affect is next to impossible. The same is true for educators who hope to install Level 3 formative assessment.

Affective inventories are not that difficult to construct, and they can supply important insights about the extent to which any shift in classroom climate has actually taken place. Almost as important, when teachers know that they will periodically administer an affective inventory dealing with classroom climate, the very prospect will usually incline them to attend more zealously to the galaxy of factors that can create the kind of classroom climate they desire.

It's been said that "we measure what we treasure." Well, for Level 3 formative assessment, where students' affect is so significant, teachers should treasure such affect enough to measure it.

climate affective inventory presented in Figure 5.4 illustrates the general strategy to be employed in such inventories. Figure 5.4's inventory is intended for middle school students, specifically for 7th graders who are taking a social studies course. Clearly, the language level and content in this example would not be appropriate for all students or all subject areas. Elementary teachers, for example, should include inventory items dealing more directly with the entire classroom rather than with any one content area.

Note in the Figure 5.4 inventory that there are four statements each that deal with the previously identified elements

Figure 5.4 | A Classroom Climate Affective Inventory

Directions: Please indicate the degree to which you agree or disagree with each of the inventory's statements by circling a letter alongside that statement. Use the following response system:

SA = Strongly Agree   A = Agree   U = Uncertain
D = Disagree   SD = Strongly Disagree

Here is a sample statement and a response:

Statement			*Response*		
During weekends, I like to watch TV.	SA	(A)	U	D	SD

Please respond honestly; there are no wrong answers. Do not put your name on the inventory or make any written comments. Your response must be completely anonymous.

1. Most students in our class take responsibility for their own social studies learning.

   SA　A　U　D　SD

2. I believe I am going to do really well in this class.

   SA　A　U　D　SD

3. Many of my classmates believe our classroom tests are really used to evaluate us.

   SA　A　U　D　SD

4. I believe our classroom assessments are used to help us learn.

   SA　A　U　D　SD

5. I think that most students in this course believe that every student will make big progress.

   SA　A　U　D　SD

6. As far as I am concerned, our teacher is really responsible for what we learn.
   SA   **A**   **U**   **D**   **SD**

7. My classmates think the teacher is totally responsible for our learning.
   SA   **A**   **U**   **D**   **SD**

8. I have doubts about whether i'll learn social studies well in this class.
   SA   **A**   **U**   **D**   **SD**

9. Students in this social studies class think that our classroom tests are used to help us learn.
   SA   **A**   **U**   **D**   **SD**

10. Classroom tests, in this class, are mostly used to give me a grade.
    SA   **A**   **U**   **D**   **SD**

11. Lots of students in this class know they're not going to do well in learning social studies.
    SA   **A**   **U**   **D**   **SD**

12. I feel personally responsible to help my classmates learn well.
    SA   **A**   **U**   **D**   **SD**

Thank you for completing this inventory.

of classroom climate: learning expectations, responsibility for learning, and the role of classroom assessment. Note also that all the odd items in the inventory (statements 1, 3, 5, 7, 9, and 11) deal with a student's perception of classmates' sentiments, whereas the even items focus on the student's own sentiments. The decision to use four items per element (resulting in a 12-item inventory) reflects the preference of the teacher who created it. For a teacher with less time to design and score inventories, or for one who has a preference for doing things as efficiently as possible, two items per element (resulting in a six-item inventory) would be a sufficient number to support a defensible inference about the students' overall status.

As you can see, the Figure 5.4 inventory contains an equal number of positively and negatively phrased statements. By assigning one to five points per statement (four points for strong agreement with a positive statement *or* four points for strong disagreement with a negative statement), a student's total score on this inventory can range from a high of 60 to a low of 12.

All such affective inventories should be carefully constructed and, ideally, taken for a test drive, perhaps with a colleague's students, before actual administration. Assuming teachers have thoughtfully developed these sorts of inventories, the occasional use of such an affective assessment device can generate useful indications of students' views of the climate present in a particular classroom and, therefore, supply evidence to support the success of Level 3 formative assessment.

SUPER-SUCCINCT SUMMARY

- Level 3 formative assessment calls for a shift from a traditional classroom climate to an assessment-informed classroom climate. Three key elements in this view of classroom climate are the teacher's and students' perceptions regarding (1) learning expectations, (2) responsibility for learning, and (3) the role of classroom assessment.

- There are five significant activities teachers should consider carrying out as part of Level 3 formative assessment: (1) distributing classroom climate guidelines, (2) seeking and nurturing trust, (3) modeling and reinforcing suitable student behavior, (4) seeking students' classroom climate suggestions, and (5) periodically assessing students' affective status regarding important classroom climate dimensions.

CHAPTER

6

Schoolwide Implementation

[Chapter Preview]

- Two practical strategies for expanding the use of formative assessment and important considerations for employing each
- What can be gained by employing these strategies in tandem

IF FORMATIVE ASSESSMENT IS A GOOD THING TO DO, THEN more teachers ought to do it. This inescapable logic is, well, inescapable.

Level 4 formative assessment involves expanding the use of Level 1, Level 2, and Level 3 formative assessment, singularly or in combination, beyond a single classroom or handful of classrooms. For example, if a principal wants to see every teacher in the school use Level 1 formative assessment, focused on teacher-adjusted instruction, then accomplishing this significant goal would constitute a clear instance of Level 4 formative assessment. And although this level usually deals with schoolwide implementation of formative assessment, the approach (and the Level 4 label) also applies to larger-scale expansion of formative assessment to entire districts, states, or provinces.

Obviously, certain levels of formative assessment are more difficult to expand than others. It would be a whole lot more challenging, for example, to install Level 3 formative assessment throughout a school than it would be to install Level 1 formative assessment in that same school. Although this *is* a book about formative assessment, and although Level 4 formative assessment deals with the expanded application of formative assessment in multiple classrooms, this is not a book about the expanded application of educational innovations. Accordingly, we will consider just two major strategies for scaling up the use of formative assessment: a *professional development strategy* and a *teacher learning community strategy*. If you wish to dig more deeply into innovation-expansion strategies, you will find several references dealing with that topic cited at the close of this book (e.g., Fullan, 2001; McLaughlin & Talbert, 2006).

Strategy 1: Professional Development

Professionals who hope to retain appropriate levels of competence need to keep learning throughout their career. Whether the professional is an attorney, a surgeon, a computer programmer, or a teacher, one fundamental tenet of professionalism is that the professional "keeps up." Those who fail to keep abreast of recent development in their field will almost certainly find themselves approaching today's tasks with yesterday's tools.

Because formative assessment constitutes a potent way for teachers to improve their own instructional effectiveness and, thereby, enhance the caliber of their students' learning, formative assessment is a justifiable focus of continuing professional development programs. To simplify a consideration of how Level 4 formative assessment's expansion orientation might function, I want to focus on *school-level* installation of one or more levels of formative assessment. Most of the principles of schoolwide expansion of educational innovations are applicable to expansions on a larger scale.

These days, we know much more about how to make professional development endeavors successful than we knew just a few decades ago. For instance, there is near-universal agreement about the ineffectiveness of visiting luminaries giving a one-shot workshop and then leaving teachers to their own devices. The reason for this is simple: Human behavior is tough to change, and one-shot workshops, even extremely illuminating and motivating ones, rarely bring about permanent changes in teachers' conduct. If a professional development program is going to have a reasonable chance of success, it must *last* over an extended period of time, *nurture* teachers who are attempting to adopt new practices, and be powerful enough to have at least a possibility to *alter* the classroom behaviors of busy teachers who are, for the most part, employing instructional procedures they've been using for years.

Accordingly, those who are planning a professional development program dealing with Level 4 formative assessment, whether they are external consultants or an internal team of educators, should focus on activities that together constitute a program of meaningful duration and potency. This program must emphasize three things: (1) definitional clarity of formative assessment; (2) the core construct of formative assessment— that is, reliance on assessment-elicited evidence to help teachers and students make improvement-focused adjustment decisions; and (3) honest appraisals of the degree to which particular procedural variations in formative assessment are supported by research and reason.

Let's consider each of these emphases in more detail.

Emphasis 1: Definitional Clarity of Formative Assessment

Any professional development program focused on formative assessment that does not promptly and completely clarify what "formative assessment" is will be seriously compromised and unlikely to succeed.

As you may imagine, my preferred definition is the one we're using in this book:

> Formative assessment is a planned process in which assessment-elicited evidence of students' status is used by teachers to adjust their ongoing instructional procedures or by students to adjust their current learning tactics.

One of the reasons I like this definition so much is that it rules out a number of actions educators might *mistakenly* believe to constitute formative assessment. Imagine, for example, that a teacher is explaining a complex concept to a class. Noticing one student's puzzled expression, the teacher decides to re-explain the complex concept. Has this teacher made an instructional adjustment? Yes. Was it a good idea? Probably. But was this teacher using formative assessment? No, and by this point in the book, I suspect you know why not: (1) the instructional adjustment was based on a visual clue—a student's apparent puzzlement—and not on *assessment-elicited evidence* and (2) the adjustment was ad hoc and not part of a *planned process*. It may have been fine instruction, but fine instruction and formative assessment are not identical. (Formative assessment is, instead, a way to make instruction finer!)

A serious attempt to make sure all professional development participants have a common understanding of what constitutes formative assessment heads off the confusion that inevitably results when different teachers bring different definitional understandings to the professional development program. Many teachers may claim, "I already do formative assessment because I adjust my teaching according to how well my students seem to be learning." We need to get many more teachers to employ formative assessment in their classrooms, and if too many teachers are allowed to believe they're "already doing it," then there will be fewer teachers likely to learn what formative assessment is all about and, therefore, adopt it.

One useful way of promoting participants' understanding of what formative assessment is, and what it isn't, is to present them with a series of fictitious vignettes, some of which are and some of which aren't consistent with the particular definition of formative assessment adopted for the professional development program. (You'll note that I presented one such mini-vignette at the beginning of this section.) Discussions of these sorts of scenarios typically help participants get a better handle on the defining characteristics of bona fide formative assessment.

It is even helpful, once participants in a professional development program have been introduced to a definition of formative assessment, to have them generate a few of their own "is/isn't" illustrations of formative assessment. Again, discussion of these illustrations can be remarkably clarifying.

Emphasis 2: The Core Construct of Formative Assessment

A second pivotal emphasis in any professional development program dealing with formative assessment is attention to the *essence* of what formative assessment really is. Because many teachers who successfully employ formative assessment have devised clever, even innovative ways of carrying out this process, there's a risk that those just learning about it may be distracted by the trappings of a particular formative assessment incarnation (and, thereafter, employ that incarnation exclusively) rather than focusing on its fundamental idea and vast potential. For example, practices involving fun or innovative ways to supply feedback to students are often worth lauding, but they may or may not be an integral component of the formative assessment process.

At bottom, formative assessment is a planned, evidence-based approach for teachers and students to improve what they're doing. Effective formative assessment arises when teachers or students or both use assessment evidence to make decisions first about whether to make improvement-aimed adjustments and then about what sorts of adjustments to make. To the uninitiated, this may seem like a fairly innocuous enterprise, but it represents the very best, *informed* decision making that can be made during instruction. Formative assessment must be seen for what it is: a high-powered, effective way to enhance students' learning that is well supported by both empirical research and common sense. There may be all sorts of glittering procedural variations to accomplish the core mission of formative assessment, but it's the core mission that matters. Be not distracted.

Emphasis 3: Candid Appraisals of Formative Assessment's Procedural Variations

A final emphasis of any first-rate professional development program dealing with formative assessment should be an honest portrayal of what we know and don't know about the efficacy of certain procedures used in connection with formative assessment. For a few of these procedures, there is reasonable empirical evidence to support the procedure's use. For other procedures, there is scant evidence attesting to their merit.

To illustrate, the topic of giving students evidence-based feedback has been researched at considerable depth during the past several decades (see, for example, Shute, 2007). Thanks to this research base, we can say with considerable confidence that teachers should supply students with assessment-based *descriptive feedback*. Descriptive feedback indicates what students can currently do and what they need to do in order to achieve a target curricular aim or master an en route building block related to that aim. Empirical research tells us that such feedback is far more effective in improving student learning than *comparative feedback,* in which a student receives only an assessment-based grade or class ranking. We know enough about the viscera of evidence-based feedback to endorse certain kinds and denigrate others.

But there are other aspects of formative assessment that are less well supported by empirical studies. For example, there aren't any studies telling us how many students must supply assessment-based evidence before a teacher should feel comfortable in making an adjustment decision. Nor are there any telling us how well a group of students must perform before a teacher should sensibly decide to adjust instruction. We are particularly bereft of evidence-based guidance regarding how to get students to take an active part in adjusting their own learning tactics or what kinds of adjustment in those tactics are apt to be most effective. And, although there is research evidence available to suggest that communicating curricular expectations to students has a positive influence on students' learning, we really do not know *how* to best communicate those expectations. One of the most compelling findings of Black and Wiliam (1998a) is that minor variations in the way teachers carry out formative assessment do not seem to get in the way of formative assessment's ultimate payoff. Yet, as these two researchers point out, we typically do not have sufficient evidence to identify *which procedural variations* of formative assessment are destined to be sure-fire winners. Research support for many formative assessment variations is simply not available at this time.

Those involved in promoting Level 4 formative assessment via a professional development strategy should be as candid as possible with their colleagues when describing different ways to carry out formative assessment in a classroom. It's perfectly all right to suggest certain procedures for teachers to employ, if they decide to give formative assessment a try, but those suggestions should always be accompanied by honest descriptions ranging from "This procedure is supported by really solid empirical evidence," all the way to "This procedure rests on nothing more solid than someone's fervent hope that it will work!" No, there's nothing wrong with a leader of a professional development program presenting and supporting instructional recommendations based only on good old-fashioned horse sense. However, if that's the rationale underlying a recommendation, then participants need to be told so. And they might even be told about the smarts of the horse involved in such thinking.

Again, professional development programs are likely to vary considerably. That's to be expected because of the different persons who design and staff the programs and the different educators these programs serve. But I want to underscore that, irrespective of what the final shape of a professional development program is, if it deals with formative assessment, it should *always* include (1) a solid dose of definitional clarity, (2) attention to formative assessment's core construct, and (3) candid appraisals of any recommended procedural variations.

MORE REALLY IS LESS

Since I retired from the UCLA faculty in the early 1990s, I've had more time to take part in a host of educational conferences, most of them dealing in one way or another with educational assessment, and all of them attended by in-the-trenches teachers and administrators. By interacting with educators at such meetings, I typically glean gobs of real-world insights about assessment from candid colleagues—insights not readily obtainable from scholarly books or journals.

One week before I wrapped up the final revision of this book, I took part in a Midwest conference dealing with the relationship between assessment and instruction. In a session dealing exclusively with the meaning of formative assessment, I saw "up close and personal" a mistake I've often seen made by the folks who provide professional development sessions for educators. The presenter had only 90 minutes and tried to cover too much content . . . way too much content.

This presenter had all sorts of good things to tell us about formative assessment. His explanations were crisp, his examples were on target, and his many, *many* handouts were well designed. But by trying to do too much, he wasted everyone's time. As the session progressed, I looked around me and noticed more and more of the educators in attendance tuning out to what was going on at the front of the room. They were overwhelmed, and so was I.

Throughout this book I've stressed that any formative assessment models seen as onerous by teachers are formative assessment models that are unlikely to be used. And unused formative assessment models won't help anybody: teachers or students. The same holds for professional development sessions about formative assessment. If you ever have access to 90 precious minutes of busy educators' time, make sure those educators carry away one or two things truly learned instead of 30 things forgotten 90 seconds after the session is over.

Strategy 2: Teacher Learning Communities

A teacher learning community (TLC) is a group of teachers who work together over an extended period to strengthen their own individual capabilities in an area of mutual interest. TLCs have become particularly popular in recent years by appealing to those teachers who wish to work with fellow teachers in sharpening their instructional, curricular, or assessment skills (Thompson & Wiliam, 2007; U.S. Department of Education, 2005).

Thompson and Wiliam (2007), while describing the role that TLCs can play in promoting more widespread use of what they call "assessment for learning" (essentially formative assessment as described here), explain why a TLC can be so useful in fostering this objective:

> There are several . . . ways that teacher learning communities seem to be particularly functional vehicles to support teacher learning about assessment for learning. First, the practice of assessment for learning depends upon a high level of professional judgment on the part of teachers, so it is consistent to build professional development around a teacher-as-local-expert model. Second, school-embedded teacher learning communities are sustained over time, allowing change to occur developmentally, which in turn increases the likelihood of the change "sticking" at both the individual and school level. Third, teacher learning communities are a non-threatening venue allowing teachers to notice weaknesses in their content knowledge and get help with these deficiencies from peers. For example, in discussing an assessment for learning practice that revolves around specific content (e.g., by examining student work that reveals student misconceptions), teachers often confront gaps in their own subject-matter knowledge, which can be remedied in conversations with their colleagues. (p. 17)

During a period when both Thompson and Wiliam were affiliated with Educational Testing Service (ETS), they worked with a group of skilled ETS collaborators to devise a well-conceived program called Keeping Learning on Track. This program's underlying strategy was assessment for learning, an approach essentially equivalent to the definition of formative assessment found in this book.

Wiliam and his ETS colleagues devised a two-stage intervention commencing with (1) an initial workshop or, preferably, several workshops focused on the innards of formative assessment, followed by (2) TLCs for workshop attendees extending over one or two years' duration. A brief description of how a TLC functions in the Keeping Learning on Track approach will provide a better idea of typical TLC particulars.

A group of teachers agrees to meet monthly for one to two years. Each meeting, lasting from 90 to 120 minutes, commences with an identification of the meeting's chief goal or intention and then is followed up quickly with a "How's it going?" segment, in which each TLC member briefly reports on relevant events that have transpired since the previous TLC meeting. After those reports, TLC members typically attempt to practice one formative assessment procedure designated for that session. For example, a session might be focused on how to frame pivotal adjustment-trigger questions presented during an ongoing class discussion and how to decide, based on students' whiteboard responses, if an instructional adjustment is warranted.

Much of a given TLC session is devoted to teachers' practicing that session's particular procedure, always selected in advance. Any of the four separate steps in Level 1 formative assessment (see p. 53) and any of the supporting actions necessary to facilitate the analogous four steps in Level 2 formative assessment (see p. 82) would be an appropriate focus for a given TLC session.

Near the close of a TLC meeting, each teacher who follows this ETS model describes the chief elements of a "Personal Action Plan" detailing what that teacher intends to try out or practice before the next TLC meeting. (Usually, those plans deal with the formative assessment procedure that was the focus of the meeting about to be concluded.) Finally, members devote several minutes to a reflective discussion of whether they actually achieved the announced goal of the meeting.

This treatment of how a TLC operates barely scratches the surface. But it should be apparent that TLCs can successfully promote Level 4 formative assessment in a school, provided that there are thoughtful ground rules for meeting conduct and between-meeting activities. A small group of, say, a half-dozen committed members of a TLC focused on formative assessment is preferable to a TLC of twice that number if half of its members are indifferent to what's going on. A core group of motivated and competent users of formative assessment can, by their enthusiastic modeling of this potent process, stimulate other colleagues to emulate them.

The Most Effective Approach: The Strategies Combined

We have, so far, considered the two strategies for accomplishing Level 4 formative assessment as though they must be separate. However, as the architects of the ETS program Keeping Learning on Track concluded, the best way to accomplish a schoolwide implementation of formative assessment is to employ *both* professional development and TLCs. After a series of orienting workshops regarding the key features of formative assessment, those teachers in a school who really wish to become skilled in formative assessment sign up for a one-year or two-year stint as a member of a TLC focused exclusively on formative assessment.

Other variations of professional development and TLCs are, of course, possible. For example, a school's TLC could start from scratch—without any upfront workshops—and use the first several meetings (monthly or more frequently, depending on the group's available time) to work through the chief contents of a book about formative assessment, such as the one you're currently reading. For example, let's say that members of a TLC have decided to deal only with the expanded use of Level 1 formative assessment and its focus on teachers' instructional adjustments. The next three meetings could deal, then, with the first three chapters of this book and move during subsequent meetings into the kind of approach designed in the Keeping Learning on Track TLC meetings.

What's important in Level 4 formative assessment is that there's a carefully conceived, well-implemented effort to get more teachers to employ this powerful process. If that goal is achieved, more students will be better educated.

SUPER–SUCCINCT SUMMARY

- Level 4 formative assessment is expanded implementation of formative assessment at the school level and beyond.

- Professional development for Level 4 formative assessment must emphasize three things: (1) definitional clarity regarding the nature of formative assessment, (2) reliance on assessment-elicited evidence to help teachers and students make improvement-focused adjustment decisions, and (3) honest appraisals of the degree to which particular procedural variations in formative assessment are supported by research and reason.

- TLCs, groups of teachers who work together over an extended period of time to strengthen their individual curricular, instructional, or assessment skills, are recommended as powerful ways for teachers to acquire insights and techniques associated with formative assessment.

- Level 4 formative assessment can best be implemented by blending of both professional development and the extended employment of TLCs.

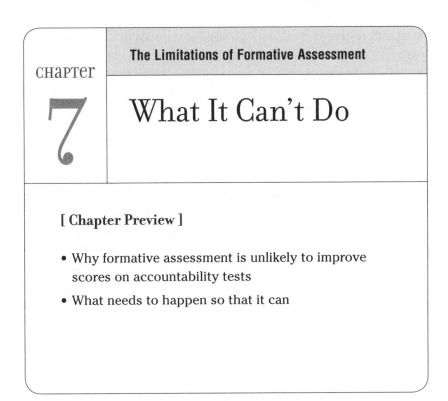

CHAPTER

7

The Limitations of Formative Assessment

What It Can't Do

[Chapter Preview]

- Why formative assessment is unlikely to improve scores on accountability tests
- What needs to happen so that it can

WAY BACK AT THE BEGINNING OF THIS BOOK, WE TALKED about how many educators have been drawn to formative assessment by the hope that this process could significantly improve students' scores on critical accountability tests. Well, let's greet the bad news without delay: *Formative assessment will not improve students' scores on most of today's accountability tests,* at least not enough to make any meaningful difference.

Is it crazy for educators to think that formative assessment is the answer to their testing dilemma? Absolutely not—not when one realizes that the chief message of the Black and Wiliam meta-analysis (1998a) is that kids who are taught in a formative assessment classroom will learn more than their counterparts who are taught in classes without formative assessment. Logically, kids who have learned more in their classrooms ought to perform better on external accountability tests than kids who have learned less. This sort of reasoning is so compelling that it's easy to see why many educators have attempted to fend off accountability test pressures by going all in with formative assessment. Unfortunately, this strategy simply won't work. Let's see why.

Different Times, Different Assessment Functions

We live in the 21st century, not the 20th. And all around us, especially in the realm of technology, there are dramatic differences between the way things were then and the way they are now. In the field of educational measurement, a profound shift in the fundamental function of large-scale (standardized) achievement testing has led to the widespread adoption of educational accountability tests that are altogether *inappropriate* for their intended evaluative function.

In the past century, the chief assessment function for large-scale, standardized tests was *comparative*. Starting shortly after World War I, standardized tests—both intelligence tests and achievement tests—were used primarily to compare test-takers with one another. Typically, these comparative interpretations were accomplished by relying on *norm-referenced* interpretations, which involve "referencing" a test-taker's test score to the scores of a previous group of representative test-takers known as the norm group. This is why, when we talk about standardized test scores, we talk about "percentiles." Saying, for instance, that 4th grader Jason scored at the 86th percentile means that his score exceeded the performance of 85 percent of the test-takers in the *norm group*. For comparative interpretations, we make sense out of an examinee's test performance by referencing it back to a norm group's performance.

Now think about the dominant role of standardized achievement tests in the *current* century. Unquestionably, it is to evaluate educational effectiveness. In the United States, for example, the No Child Left Behind Act (NCLB) was enacted in 2002 as an accountability-focused school improvement law in which individual schools were to be evaluated on the basis of their students' scores on state-selected standardized achievement tests.

What's important to understand is that achievement tests built for a comparative assessment function are altogether *unsuitable* for fulfilling a school-evaluation function. The sad reality is that almost all of today's educational accountability tests are *instructionally insensitive*, incapable of detecting the difference between effective and ineffective instruction. Even sadder is the fact that so few educators realize this reality. When an instructionally insensitive test is used as an accountability test, the bulk of learning benefits from classroom formative assessment simply won't show up in the test results. Although powerful learning has occurred, the instructionally insensitive tests are incapable of measuring and documenting it.

Instructionally Insensitive Accountability Tests

In the United States today, almost all educational accountability tests are of two varieties: *traditional standardized achievement tests* and *customized standards-based tests*. Both of these types of tests are standardized in the sense that they are administered, scored, and interpreted in a standard, predetermined manner. For decisively different reasons, both these kinds of accountability tests are unable to accurately detect the quality of instruction (Popham, 2007) or pick up the learning improvements that formative assessment brings about. Let's consider the two types of tests in turn and why each is instructionally insensitive.

Traditional Standardized Achievement Tests

Standardized achievement tests have been with us for a long time and have passed on from generation to generation virtually untouched in design and mission. Today's standardized achievement tests trace their roots to the Army Alpha test, a standardized aptitude test comparing potential officer candidates in

World War I. Nationally standardized achievement tests made their first appearance a few years after that war, and the fact that the Stanford Achievement Tests, first published in 1923, are currently in their 10th edition attests to U.S. educators' continued demand for this kind of testing. Other examples of traditional standardized achievement tests are the Iowa Tests of Basic Skills, the California Achievement Tests, and the Terra Nova achievement tests.

In many states, one of these four standardized tests has been chosen as the state's official accountability test, required by NCLB. More often than not, these states have added new test items to the off-the-shelf test to better align the test with state curricular emphases. However, the essential function of a traditional standardized achievement test, even one augmented with more items and employed for accountability purposes, is to permit comparative score interpretations among test-takers.

Lest it seem like I'm picking on comparative score-interpretations, I should note that these are altogether appropriate in any sort of fixed-quota circumstance when there are more applicants than openings and the mission is to whittle the applicant pool to the appropriate size. During most of the 20th century, this was the chief reason educators administered standardized achievement tests to students: to find out who was "better" or "worse" than whom. The way this works is by setting up a test so that test-takers will generate a substantial range of scores: some high scores, some low scores, and a flock of middling scores. With this *score-spread* established, it's possible to make fine-grained contrasts among different students' scores. If there is an insufficient score-spread, then traditional standardized achievement tests simply don't work the way they are intended to work.

To create sufficient score-spread on a traditional standardized achievement test, roughly half of the test-takers should be able to answer the vast majority of the test's items correctly. The percentage of students who answer a given item correctly is referred to as the item's p-*value*. Thus, an item answered correctly by 50 percent of students would have a *p*-value of .50.

Statistically speaking, items that are the best contributors to a test's overall score-spread are those that have *p*-values between .40 and .60. Items that are answered correctly by too many students (e.g., an item with a *p*-value of .90) or by too few students (e.g., an item with a *p*-value of .10) do not contribute their share to generating the spread in students' scores so coveted by the builders of standardized achievement tests.

An instructionally sensitive accountability test would be one that would include many items that *uninstructed* students would tend to answer incorrectly and *instructed* students would tend to answer correctly. But educators must realize that the developers of traditional standardized achievement tests have no interest in building tests to measure instructional quality. Remember, traditional standardized achievement tests are designed to produce comparative score interpretations, not determine instructional success. As long as a traditional standardized achievement test is capable of creating sufficient score-spread, then comparative interpretations can be made, and the test will do its job. But, unfortunately, some of the ways that developers of standardized achievement tests generate score-spread render those tests instructionally insensitive. Let's see why.

Socioeconomic-linked items. Because the creation of score-spread is such a powerful goal of those who build standardized achievement tests, they link many items to students' *socioeconomic status* (SES). If you were to spend just a few minutes looking carefully at the items in any traditional standardized achievement test, you would most certainly identify a number of items that students from higher SES backgrounds will be more likely to answer correctly than would students from lower SES backgrounds. Several years ago, I spent quite a lot of time examining traditional standardized tests and identified many such items. You will find several examples in Chapter 4 of *The Truth About Testing* (Popham, 2001).

To provide a quick illustration, consider a science item on a 6th grade standardized achievement test that first explains that a plant's fruit contains seeds and then asks test-takers to identify which of the following is not a fruit—apple, pumpkin, orange, or celery. Children who regularly eat fresh apples and oranges, snack on celery sticks, and carve pumpkins into jack-o'-lanterns every Halloween are more likely to answer this item correctly than are children whose parents rely on food stamps to feed the family and can't afford the luxury of fresh fruit and vegetables, let alone a $12 pumpkin for jack-o'-lantern carving. Does celery contain seeds? Does a pumpkin? Students who have never eaten celery or seen the inside of a pumpkin will have to guess. Although the bias is subtle, the inclusion of such content in a standardized test's items tends to penalize children from less affluent backgrounds.

Because SES is a variable that's nicely spread out, and a variable that doesn't change all that rapidly, the more SES-linked items there are in a traditional standardized achievement test, the more likely it is that the test will produce a substantial degree of score-spread. But SES-linked items measure what students *brought* to school, not what students were *taught* in school. SES-linked items contribute to a standardized achievement test's instructional insensitivity. The more such items there are on an accountability test, the less instructionally sensitive the test will be.

Aptitude-linked items. Another kind of item that's often used in traditional standardized achievement tests to generate score-spread is an item linked to students' *inherited academic aptitude*. Thanks to the gene pool lottery, students differ from birth in the degree of verbal aptitude, quantitative aptitude, and spatial aptitude they possess. (Although they may certainly develop strong skills in these areas and achieve great academic success, it will take them longer to do so and require more effort.)

Lots of standardized achievement tests feature items that obviously measure not curricular content but verbal, quantitative, and spatial aptitude. You can find several of these items in Chapter 4 of *The Truth About Testing* as well. A typical example is an item for which a correct answer requires the student to mentally invert or reverse some sort of three-dimensional geometric shape. Students who were born with ample "spatial smarts" will be able to handle this task easily; those whose inborn "spatial smarts" are skimpy will have a much tougher time. Again, though, items linked to inherited quantitative, verbal, or spatial aptitudes measure what students bring to school, not what they are taught once they arrive. The more such items there are on a traditional standardized achievement test, the less instruction-ally sensitive the test will be.

When the people who build traditional standardized achieve-ment tests set out to do so, they always include items likely to contribute to a test's score-spread. Moreover, each time the test is revised, as all current tests of this sort are, items that do not contribute to score-spread—namely, items the majority of stu-dents answer correctly—will be jettisoned. What this means is that, over time, more and more SES-linked items and aptitude-linked items will make their way into the tests, making oft-revised standardized achievement tests increasingly insensitive to instruction.

I must pause now to stress that the builders of traditional standardized achievement tests are not malevolent villains who set out to penalize children from low-SES families or children whose innate aptitudes aren't terrific. Rather, those test-builders are simply trying to create tests that do a good job of spreading out test-takers' scores. But what makes a test great at generating comparisons often makes it terrible at detecting the signs of effective or ineffective instruction. If a school's student body is composed largely of high-SES children who happen to possess substantial inherited academic aptitudes, then that school's stu-dents will tend to score well on standardized achievement tests *regardless of how effectively they were taught.* And if a school's student body is composed largely of low-SES children who hap-pen to possess weaker inherited academic aptitudes, then that school's students will tend to score poorly on standardized achievement tests, again, *regardless of how effectively they were taught.*

What this means for educators who use formative assess-ment is that the in-class learning gains flowing from the use of assessment evidence to adjust instructional approaches and learning tactics are highly unlikely to translate into dramatically higher scores on traditional standardized achievement tests. Oh, there may be modest improvements; after all, students who are able to read and understand a test item have a much better chance of answering it correctly than students who can't. But if the accountability test being used is a traditional standardized achievement test, even one that's been supplemented for closer alignment with state standards, the instructional insensitivity of this type of test means even spectacular formative assessment is unlikely to send students' scores soaring.

Customized Standards-Based Tests

The second widely used type of accountability test is a *customized standards-based test*. Roughly half of the states in the United States have adopted this kind of test as their NCLB accountability test. Simply put, a customized standards-based test is a test built to measure the degree to which students have mastered a state's *content standards*, its officially authorized curricular aims. Although different states employ different labels to describe their curricular aims (e.g., benchmarks, expectancies, goals, or objectives), when a test is specifically constructed to gauge students' status with regard to those curricular aims, that test is a customized standards-based test.

Although the idea of standards-based tests represents fundamental sound logic, there is a serious conceptual mistake that prevents almost all these tests from functioning as the education community wants them to function. Interestingly, this conceptual shortcoming is not a measurement mistake, but a *curricular* one.

Too many curricular targets. There's not time enough to teach everything educators would like their students to learn. Similarly, there's not time enough to *test* everything educators would like to know if their students have learned. Educators in the United States should have discovered this truth during the 1960s and 1970s, when federally advocated "behavioral objectives" were widespread in schools. Behavioral objectives described the post-instruction behaviors that students were supposed to display, and educators were urged to be as specific as possible in spelling out the nature of these sought-for post-instruction behaviors. Here's an example: "The student will be able to correctly match one-sentence written definitions with names of the eight parts of speech." The problem with such behavioral objectives was that they were far too specific and, as a result, were far too numerous. Teachers, overwhelmed by excessive numbers of behavioral objectives, simply disregarded them.

Yet, despite the well-warranted collapse of the behavioral objectives movement a generation earlier, when curriculum specialists in the 1990s began to identify the curricular goals (now called "content standards") that they wanted their students to learn, they went overboard in exactly the same way. Today, reviewing any state's official content standards (which are typically accompanied by subsets of more specific curricular aims called benchmarks, performance objectives, or the like) can take an entire day or, in some states, an entire week. The inevitable conclusion is that there are too many targets. What states have are more wish lists on the part of their curricular architects than a realistic set of curricular goals for teachers to teach or for assessors to assess. In many states, you'll find that an elementary teacher is supposed to teach students to master *literally* hundreds of state-dictated curricular aims during a nine-month school year. In mathematics or in language arts, you might find more than 100 curricular aims eligible to be assessed on a state's annual accountability test. This may sound admirable, but the kicker is that the annual accountability test must be completed in a mere 60 minutes.

Given those enormous numbers of curricular aims, it is patently impossible to measure students' mastery of all such aims on a given year's accountability test. The assessment personnel in a state's department of education, facing the measurement impossibility of too many things to be tested in too little time, typically decide to *sample* the curricular aims to be assessed in a given year. There really is no other viable choice. But because this year's upcoming accountability test is likely to assess different curricular aims than last year's accountability test, teachers who want their students to perform well on an approaching accountability test are obliged to *guess* about what's actually going to be measured. Sometimes teachers will guess correctly, meaning they will have emphasized in their classes the curricular aims that turn out to be assessed on a particular end-of-year accountability test. But, given the huge number of curricular aims eligible for assessment, *more often than not, teachers will guess incorrectly* and will have emphasized curricular aims that aren't on the test at all. After a few years of off-target instructional guessing, many teachers simply stop paying attention, in a test-preparation sense, to the skills and knowledge embodied in the state's too-numerous collections of curricular aims. In short, if you are teacher who uses formative assessment to help your students realize great gains in curriculum mastery, you may get lucky and see those gains reflected in customized standards based test scores. But don't count on it.

Dysfunctional reporting of results. Another difficulty stemming from the profusion of curricular aims that customized standards-based tests try to assess is that the tests themselves can't possibly include a sufficient number of items to shed light on a students' status regarding the curricular aims that do make the cut in a given year. More often than not, there's only one item, or perhaps two, to assess students' achievement of a specific curricular aim. Teachers really can't get an accurate fix on a student's mastery of a curricular aim based on only one or two items. Typically, the developers of customized standards-based accountability tests report students' performances at more general levels of aggregation: amalgamations of students' performance with respect to collections of a variety of curricular aims, some of them very different. This is what you see when accountability results are reported at the "strand" level or at the "content standard" level. But this kind of reporting obfuscates *which* curricular aims students have mastered. As a consequence, teachers really can't tell which aims they've taught well and which they've taught poorly. The test results provide no help to teachers for improving next year's instructional plans because the quality of this year's instruction *per curricular aim* has been shrouded by excessively general reporting systems.

Once more, after a few years of teachers' gaining no insights from these sorts of dysfunctional reporting schemes, many teachers simply give up on getting anything instructionally useful out of their state's customized standards-based accountability tests. And when teachers who are afflicted with an instructionally insensitive standards-based test really toss in the towel, guess which two variables end up primarily contributing to students' scores on these well-intentioned but warped accountability tests? If you guessed the two variables were students' SES and their inherited academic aptitudes, you win.

EXCEPTIONS ARE, BY DEFINITION, EXCEPTIONAL

I now live in Oregon, about a half-hour from where I was born in Portland many years ago. Contrary to the allegations of several of my friends, at the time of my birth Oregon had emerged from territorial status and had actually become a state.

Although there are differences in the way states deal with the reporting of a school's students' scores on accountability tests, Oregon's approach is fairly typical. Each fall, a few weeks before Halloween, the local papers carry front-page stories and school-by-school score breakdowns on the various tests administered near the tail-end of the previous academic year. Schools and districts that haven't made sufficient progress are identified as such, and these "failing" schools and districts garner most of the media attention.

Almost without exception, among these school-by-school reports there will be several schools where test scores are quite high even though a school's students are drawn from lower SES groups. These schools, often labeled as "effective" or "high-achieving" schools, seem to contradict my warnings about inappropriate, instructionally insensitive accountability tests. If these schools can get students' scores to be much higher than those of schools with similar student bodies, why can't all schools boost their students' scores?

Colleagues have raised this question to me more than a few times. Indeed, just a week ago I received an e-mail from a friend asking how, given the presence of instructionally insensitive tests, some schools in his state were able to outperform schools whose students were much more affluent. I replied to my friend that he needs to think about "the rule rather than the exception." If there is a school headed by a genuinely superlative principal, staffed by skilled and caring teachers, and with loads of support from almost all of the school's parents, it may be possible to raise students' scores even on a blatantly insensitive accountability test. But this will be the exception, not the rule.

When a state's accountability test is loaded with items that more affluent kids have a higher likelihood of answering correctly than less affluent kids, then the vast majority of the state's schools will be unable to raise their students' scores enough to make a difference, even if those students have been well taught. Just as unfortunate, when an instructionally insensitive accountability test is being used, many schools serving high-SES kids will appear to be doing a good instructional job when, in fact, this may not be the case. And so it is that inappropriate accountability tests, except for an aberrant few instances, supply a misleading picture of a school's instructional effectiveness.

Appropriate Accountability Tests

Although it is comforting to know the dividends of formative assessment will show up in the ways that really matter most—namely, in the classroom—practical-minded educators can't help but hope for a way to officially document instructional improvement and learning gains. There is a glimmer hope. The gains achieved through formative assessment could show up on external achievement examinations, provided that those examinations are designed to be both instructionally supportive and instructionally sensitive (Popham, 2007). Such tests must possess four attributes, each of which I will now briefly describe.

Attribute 1: A Modest Number of Extraordinarily Important Curricular Aims

An appropriate accountability test measures students' mastery of only an intellectually manageable and instructionally accomplishable set of curricular outcomes. Because "space" is limited, these curricular aims must be incontestably important. Thus, an appropriate accountability test in reading might assess students' mastery of only 7 or 8 curricular aims rather than 30 or 40, but those chosen aims will be truly high-level, challenging outcomes.

The curricular aims measured by an appropriate accountability test must be crafted with considerable care so that each such aim subsumes a number of lesser subskills and bodies of knowledge, but such subsumption does not obscure the nature of the curricular aim itself. Here is an example of a properly framed curricular aim:

> Students will be able to compose high-quality narrative, expository, persuasive, or descriptive essays.

This is a single curricular aim covering four different genres of composition, each of which contains a number of subskills and bodies of enabling knowledge. But the curricular aim is eminently assessable (using students' writing samples), and it is eminently teachable.

Attribute 2: Clear Descriptions of the Assessed Curricular Aims

An appropriate accountability test must be accompanied by lucid descriptions of each skill or body of knowledge that it will assess. These descriptions also require careful crafting. They must be relatively brief and written in teacher-palatable language and should be accompanied by a few sample items for purposes of illustration. Properly constructed assessment descriptions make it possible for teachers to aim their instruction at helping students achieve generalizable mastery of the skills and bodies of knowledge being assessed rather than at helping students provide the correct answers to a set of specific test items.

For a teacher who uses formative assessment, the enhanced clarity about the nature of a curricular aim that a properly devised assessment description provides can make instructional preparation a lot easier. Knowing exactly what students are supposed to know and be able to do at the end of instruction supports better decision making about the initial design of instruction, as well as the creation of learning progressions and en route assessments.

Attribute 3: Per-Student, Per-Curricular-Aim Reports

The third attribute of an appropriate accountability test is a reporting system that provides each student with a description of his or her performance related to every curricular aim that is assessed. Depending on the breadth of the curricular aim, experienced teachers should be able to identify the minimum number of test items that would be sufficient to provide a reasonably accurate per-aim estimate of a student's curricular-aim status. Sometimes this might be accomplished using only 5 or 6 items for certain aims; for other curricular aims 10 or more items might be needed. The requirement to supply a per-aim report for each student is a sensible and defensible way to determine the number of curricular aims that the test covers overall. Using enough items to measure a student's status regarding each curricular aim naturally limits the number of curricular aims an accountability test can measure with any meaningful degree of accuracy.

Given these per-aim reports, teachers can ascertain the effectiveness of their current year's teaching and can then, if certain segments of their instruction seem less than lustrous, make changes in their next year's lesson plans. (And yes, you will by now no doubt recognize that although this lesson plan revision would be a superb action to take, it would not be a part of the formative assessment process because it does not occur as part of the teacher's *ongoing* instruction to the same group of students.)

Before looking at the fourth attribute of an appropriate accountability test, let's consider the three attributes of such tests we've considered so far, namely, (1) assessment of a modest number of super-important curricular aims, (2) clear descriptions of what's to be assessed, and (3) per-curricular-aim reports for every student. Taken together, these three attributes are necessary for an accountability test to be *instructionally supportive.* A few months before the enactment of the No Child Left Behind Act, a national study group called the Commission on Instructionally Supportive Assessment (2001) published a report advocating for the wider use of accountability tests that possess the three aforementioned attributes and referring to such assessments as "instructionally supportive accountability tests." Commission members believed that accountability tests possessing these three attributes would stimulate educators' improved instruction. The state of Wyoming, incidentally, has attempted to build its state accountability tests so that they are instructionally supportive.

But, regrettably, an instructionally *supportive* accountability test might not be instructionally *sensitive*, and it really should be if it is going to be an appropriate accountability test. We have talked about an instructionally sensitive test being one capable of detecting the effectiveness of instruction. Here's a more comprehensive definition that, though a mite formal, will help clarify the difference between tests that are instructionally supportive and those that are instructionally sensitive:

> *Instructional sensitivity:* The degree to which students' performances on a test accurately reflect the quality of instruction specifically provided to promote students' mastery of what is being assessed.

You see, even if an accountability test is built so it measures a modest number of super-important curricular aims, clearly describes what's to be measured, and supplies every student with reports on each curricular aim measured, *it might still be instructionally insensitive!* Students' test scores arise from the way students respond to the items on a test, and a test's items can be more or less sensitive to the detection of instructional quality. And this is why, in order for an accountability test to be truly appropriate, there's a fourth attribute that such a test must possess.

Attribute 4: Instructionally Sensitive Items

An appropriate accountability test will contain a substantial number of items that can help us determine whether the students responding to the test have been effectively taught. If, for instance, a teacher is trying to get students to acquire a powerful cognitive skill, then an instructionally sensitive item related to that skill would be one that a student who has mastered the skill would likely respond to correctly, while a student who has not mastered the skill would have trouble. Instructionally sensitive items, therefore, not only need to be "aligned," in a loose sense, to a curricular aim that's being taught but must also deal with the central rather than peripheral aspect of whatever is embodied in that curricular aim.

How can we tell if an accountability test's items are instructionally sensitive? Well, there are two strategies for doing so, namely, using either a judgmental strategy or an empirical strategy. *Judgmental strategies* call for items to be reviewed, one item at a time, by well-trained judges. *Empirical strategies* require items to be tried out in actual instructional settings.

Judgmental strategies. To tell if the items on an accountability test are likely to be instructionally sensitive, a group of item-reviewers could be asked to render a Yes, No, or Not Sure response to review questions such as these:

• *SES influence:* Would a student's likelihood of responding correctly to this item be dominantly determined by the socio-economic status of the student's family?

• *Inherited academic aptitudes:* Would a student's likelihood of responding correctly to this item be dominantly determined by the student's innate verbal, quantitative, or spatial aptitudes?

• *Responsiveness to instruction:* If a teacher has provided reasonably effective instruction related to what's measured by this item, is it likely a substantial majority of the teacher's students will respond correctly to the item?

An instructionally sensitive item would be one that garnered mostly negative judgments from reviewers on the first two questions and mostly positive judgments on the third question. An accountability test containing many items judged to be instructionally sensitive is likely to be more appropriate that one containing few such items.

Empirical strategies. The instructional sensitivity of a test's items could also be gauged through actual tryouts: contrasting the responses of "taught" students with the responses of "untaught" students. This might be as simple as administering the same items before and after a unit of study, comparing students' performances, and identifying those items where there were meaningful pre- to post-test improvements. Similarly, items could be administered to two different groups of students, one of which had been taught whatever is being assessed by the items and one of which has not. Again, the analysis would attempt to identify items on which there were striking performance differences in favor of the taught students.

As you can see, these two strategies can be used separately or in tandem. What's most important, of course, is that there is a deliberate effort to enhance the instructional sensitivity of an accountability test's items. If the test itself is instructionally *supportive*, and the bulk of its items are instructionally *sensitive*, then you have an accountability test that is, indeed, *appropriate*.

Formative Assessment: Use It or Pass It By?

Although formative assessment is a wonderful, research-rooted way for teachers to teach better and for learners to learn better, it is unlikely to make much of a difference when it comes to increasing students' scores on inappropriate accountability tests, especially those that are instructionally insensitive, and thus, it is unlikely to change the way a school's instructional staff are evaluated. Should this drawback discourage anyone from using formative assessment or advocating its use? You should be able to guess my answer to that sort of question.

Because instructionally inappropriate accountability tests not only fail to supply an accurate evaluation of school quality but also may lead some teachers to engage in student-harmful instructional practices, such as excessive test-preparation or the elimination of curricular content deemed unlikely to be assessed by an accountability test, educators should actively advocate that these tests be replaced with accountability tests that are unequivocally appropriate. It's these tests that will be able to capture formative assessment's profoundly positive impact on students' learning and communicate what it can do: to other educators, to parents, to the public, and to influential decision makers. The more successful formative assessment is seen to be, the more frequently it will be adopted and, over time, retained. And, as a consequence, the better off learners will be.

SUPER-SUCCINCT SUMMARY

- Traditional standardized achievement tests are designed to create score spread to permit comparative representations. They often achieve this end by using items linked to students' socioeconomic status and to their inherited academic aptitudes, and these items tend to make such tests instructionally insensitive.

- Customized standards-based tests attempt to measure students' status with respect to too many curricular aims and typically measure the composition of a school's student body rather than a teaching staff's effectiveness.

- An instructionally supportive test (1) measures a modest number of truly important curricular aims, (2) provides clear description of the skills or knowledge measured, and (3) supplies all students with reports regarding each curricular aim assessed.

- An instructionally sensitive test accurately detects the quality of instruction specifically provided to promote students' mastery of what is being assessed.

- Formative assessment is likely to have a substantial impact on students' performance *only on appropriate accountability tests*, namely, those that are both instructionally supportive and instructionally sensitive.

A Visual Epilogue

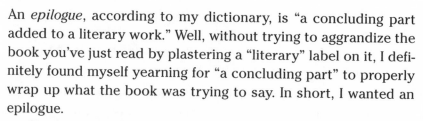

An *epilogue*, according to my dictionary, is "a concluding part added to a literary work." Well, without trying to aggrandize the book you've just read by plastering a "literary" label on it, I definitely found myself yearning for "a concluding part" to properly wrap up what the book was trying to say. In short, I wanted an epilogue.

But I am, at heart, a visually oriented person, so I opted for a final graphic that would capture the conception of formative assessment presented in the book. I hope you'll spend just a moment or two taking a gander at this graphic. I think it will help you get an accurate idea of what's involved when formative assessment is conceived of as a multilevel enterprise built atop learning progressions aimed at students' mastery of target curricular aims.

What you'll see represented in this visual epilogue is really quite straightforward. Formative assessment is a process whereby assessment-elicited evidence is used by teachers to improve their ongoing instruction or by students to improve

The Four Levels of **Formative Assessment**

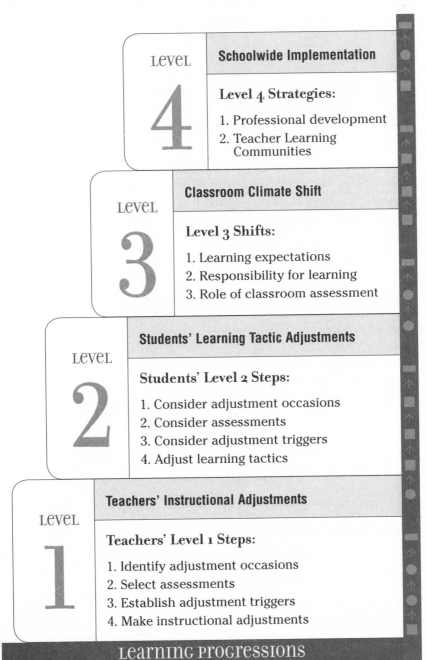

LEVEL

4

Schoolwide Implementation

Level 4 Strategies:

1. Professional development
2. Teacher Learning
   Communities

LEVEL

3

Classroom Climate Shift

Level 3 Shifts:

1. Learning expectations
2. Responsibility for learning
3. Role of classroom assessment

LEVEL

2

Students' Learning Tactic Adjustments

Students' Level 2 Steps:

1. Consider adjustment occasions
2. Consider assessments
3. Consider adjustment triggers
4. Adjust learning tactics

LEVEL

1

Teachers' Instructional Adjustments

Teachers' Level 1 Steps:

1. Identify adjustment occasions
2. Select assessments
3. Establish adjustment triggers
4. Make instructional adjustments

Learning Progressions

how they're trying to learn something. What does *not* come through in the visual, however, are two really important points, both of which I've stressed in the book. The first of these is that formative assessment, when appropriately employed, helps kids learn better—but it won't do so if it's not used. Therefore, it is imperative for formative assessment not to be presented or interpreted as something so complicated or so time-consuming that teachers simply won't use it. A second point that's impossible to represent visually (at least for me) is the enormous potential of the formative assessment process to change the way a teacher *thinks* about instruction. Formative assessment can become the catalyst that spurs both teachers and students to routinely make *evidence-based decisions* about learning. Such an orientation to teaching and learning will almost certainly improve students' learning.

As you see, formative assessment has different levels, each of which involves different activities. But the overriding gestalt my visual tries to convey is that formative assessment need not be all that complicated. What this assessment approach to evidence-based decision making can do, of course, is *transform* the way a teacher teaches.

Resources

Author's Note: Starred references are particularly useful for practitioners.

*Black, P., & Wiliam, D. (1998a). Assessment and classroom learning. *Assessment in Education: Principles, Policy and Practice, 5*(1), 7–73.

*Black, P., & Wiliam, D. (1998b, October). Inside the black box: Raising standards through classroom assessment. *Phi Delta Kappan, 80*(2), 139–149.

Bloom, B. S. (1969). Some theoretical issues relating to educational evaluation. In R. W. Taylor (Ed.), *Educational evaluation: New roles, new means: The 68th yearbook of the National Society for the Study of Education, Part II* (pp. 26–50). Chicago: University of Chicago Press.

Commission on Instructionally Supportive Assessment. (2001, October). Building tests to support instruction and accountability: A guide for policymakers. Washington, DC: National Education Association. Available: http://www.nea.org/accountability/buildingtests.html

Crooks, T. (1988). The impact of classroom evaluation practices on students. *Review of Educational Research, 58*(4), 438–481.

Forster, M., & Masters, G. (1996). *Assessment resource kit.* Melbourne: Australian Council for Educational Research.

Fullan, M. (2001). *Leading in a culture of change.* San Francisco: Jossey-Bass.

*Heritage, M. (2007, October). *Learning progressions: Supporting instruction and formative assessment* (Draft paper). Washington, DC: Council of Chief School Officers.

*Leahy, S., Lyon, C., Thompson, M., & Wiliam, D. (2005, November). Classroom assessment that keeps learning on track minute-by-minute, day-by-day. *Educational Leadership, 63*(3), 19–24.

*McLaughlin, M., & Talbert, J. E. (2006). *Building school-based teacher learning communities: Professional strategies to improve student achievement.* New York: Teachers College Press.

Natriello, G. (1987). The impact of evaluation processes on students. *Educational Psychologist, 22*(2), 155–175.

Popham, W. J. (2001). *The truth about testing: An educator's call to action.* Alexandria, VA: Association for Supervision and Curriculum Development.

Popham, W. J. (2003). *Test better, teach better: The instructional role of assessment.* Alexandria, VA: Association for Supervision and Curriculum Development.

Popham, W. J. (2006). *Mastering assessment: A self-service system for educators: Assessing students' affect.* New York: Routledge.

Popham, W. J. (2007, October). Instructional insensitivity of tests: Accountability's dire drawback. *Phi Delta Kappan, 89*(2), 146–150, 155.

Popham, W. J. (2008). *Classroom assessment: What teachers need to know* (5th ed.). Boston: Allyn and Bacon.

Scriven, M. (1967). The methodology of evaluation. In R. W. Tyler, R. M. Gagne, and M. Scriven (Eds.), *Perspectives of curriculum evaluation, Volume I* (pp. 39–83). Chicago: Rand McNally.

Shute, V. J. (2007). *Focus on formative feedback.* (ETS Research Report No. RR-07-11). Princeton, NJ: Educational Testing Service.

Thompson, M., & Wiliam, D. (2007, April). *Tight but loose: A conceptual framework for scaling up school reforms.* Paper presented at the annual meeting of the American Educational Research Association, Chicago.

U.S. Department of Education. (2005). Highly qualified teachers: Improving teacher quality state grants. *ESEA Title II, Part A—Non-Regulatory Guidance.* Washington, DC: Author.

Wiliam, D. (2007). Keeping learning on track: Classroom assessment and the regulation of learning. In F. K. Lester Jr. (Ed.), *Second handbook of research on mathematics teaching and learning: A project of the National Council of Teachers of Mathematics* (pp. 1053–1098). Greenwich, CT: Information Age Publishing.

Index

Note: An *f* after a page number indicates reference to a figure.

About the Author

W. James Popham is Emeritus Professor in the UCLA Graduate School of Education and Information Studies. He has spent most of his career as a teacher, largely at UCLA, where for nearly 30 years he taught courses in instructional methods for prospective teachers and graduate-level courses in evaluation and measurement. At UCLA he won several distinguished teaching awards, and in January 2000, he was recognized by *UCLA Today* as one of UCLA's top 20 professors of the 20th century.

In 1968, Dr. Popham established IOX Assessment Associates, a research and development group that created statewide student achievement tests for a dozen states. In 2002 the National Council on Measurement in Education presented him with its Award for Career Contributions to Educational Measurement. He is a former president of the American Educational Research Association (AERA) and the founding editor of *Educational Evaluation and Policy Analysis,* AERA's quarterly journal. In 2006 he was awarded a Certificate of Recognition by the National Association of Test Directors.

Dr. Popham is the author of 30 books, 200 journal articles, 50 research reports, and nearly 200 papers presented before research societies. His most recent books are *Classroom Assessment: What Teachers Need to Know, 5th Ed.* (2008); *Assessment for Educational Leaders* (2006); *Mastering Assessment: A Self-Service System for Educators* (2006); *America's "Failing" Schools: How Parents and Teachers Can Cope with No Child Left Behind* (2005); *Test Better, Teach Better: The Instructional Role of Assessment* (2003); and *The Truth About Testing: An Educator's Call to Action* (2001).